TRADE YOUR WAY TO
FREEDOM

Retire Sooner with More Money and Less Fear

Dennis Wilborn

Big Light Books

Meridian, ID

1st Ed. 2023 Published by:
Big Light Books
1740 E Fairview Ave #82
Meridian, ID 83642

Cover design by MD Emon

Disclaimers: This publication is designed to provide accurate and authoritative information in regard to the subject matter covered. It is sold with the understanding that neither the author nor the publisher is engaged in rendering legal, investment, accounting or other professional services. While the publisher and author have used their best efforts in preparing this book, they make no representations or warranties with respect to the accuracy or completeness of the contents of this book and specifically disclaim any implied warranties of merchantability or fitness for a particular purpose. No warranty may be created or extended by sales representatives or written sales materials. The advice and strategies contained herein may not be suitable for your situation. You should consult with a professional when appropriate. Neither the publisher nor the author shall be liable for any loss of profit or any other commercial damages, including but not limited to special, incidental, consequential, personal, or other damages.

U.S. Government Required Disclaimer – Commodity Futures Trading Commission: All trading has large potential rewards, but also large potential risk. You must be aware of the risks and be willing to accept them in order to invest in the futures and options markets. Don't trade with money you can't afford to lose. This is neither a solicitation nor an offer to Buy/Sell stocks, futures or options. No representation is being made that any account will or is likely to achieve profits or losses similar to those discussed in this training. The past performance of any trading system or methodology is not necessarily indicative of future results. CFTC RULE 4.41 – Hypothetical or simulated performance results have certain limitations. Unlike an actual performance record, simulated results do not represent actual trading. Also, since the trades have not been executed, the results may have under-or-over compensated for the impact, if any, of certain market factors, such as lack of liquidity. Simulated trading programs in general are also subject to the fact that they are designed with the benefit of hindsight. No representation is being made that any account will or is likely to achieve profit or losses similar to those shown. All Materials presented are for training purposes only. Traders should paper trade any new method prior to risk of personal capital.

Affiliate Disclosure: AutoPilotTraders.com is a participant in the Amazon Services LLC Associates Program, an affiliate advertising program designed to provide a means for sites to earn advertising fees by advertising and linking to Amazon.com. AutoPilot Trading may also participates in affiliate programs with Clickbank, ShareASale, and other sites. AutoPilot Trading is compensated for referring traffic and business to these companies.

Print Layout © 2017 BookDesignTemplates.com

Charts in this work are used under Fair Use standards for commentary and education.

Trade Your Way to Freedom/ Dennis Wilborn. -- 1st ed.

For everyone who dreams of freedom

Trust in the Lord with all your heart
and lean not on your own understanding;
in all your ways submit to him,
and he will make your paths straight.
—PROVERBS 3:5-6

CONTENTS

FOREWORD

In *Trade Your Way to Freedom*, Dennis Wilborn, a seasoned trader, coach, and educator, generously shares his profound insights and vast experience in the world of trading. This book is a treasure trove of knowledge, offering a roadmap not just to financial freedom but also to a more profound understanding of the art and science of trading. One of my biggest takeaways was how once you have the skills down, you can automate a LOT of the trading processes. The key is to persevere to get yourself there.

Trading can be a complex and daunting endeavor, particularly for those embarking on this journey for the first time. Dennis understands this better than most, and in this book, he simplifies the intricate web of trading strategies and principles into a format that is accessible and digestible for traders at all levels.

Beginners will find a solid foundation on which to build their trading careers. Dennis' ability to break down complex concepts into straightforward, actionable steps is a game-changer. Whether you're learning the basics of technical analysis, risk management, or trade management, this book is a fantastic starting point.

For seasoned professionals, the value of *Trade Your Way to Freedom* is equally substantial. In my experience, even the most accomplished traders benefit from continuous learning. Dennis's book is packed with strategies and tactics that can enhance your existing skill set. I, too, found new tips and tricks that will help me automate certain aspects of my trading process, ultimately saving valuable time and resources.

One of the most remarkable aspects of this book is Dennis's unwavering commitment to helping others succeed in their trading endeavors. He brings a level of dedication and mentorship to his writing that is rarely seen in the world of trading education. As you read these pages, you'll sense that you're not just learning from an expert but also from a trusted guide who genuinely cares about your success.

I've had the privilege of knowing Dennis for years, and his dedication to the trading community is evident not only in his writing but also in his coaching and education. He has been instrumental in helping countless individuals achieve their trading goals, and his students speak highly of the transformative impact he has had on their trading journeys.

Trade Your Way to Freedom is not just a book; it's a roadmap to financial independence, a guide to mastering the markets, and a testament to the power of knowledge and dedication. It's a resource that will empower you to take control of your financial future and guide you toward the freedom you desire.

As you embark on this transformative journey, remember that trading is a continuous learning process, and this book is a valuable companion on that path. Dive into its pages, absorb the wisdom it imparts, and let it be the catalyst for your journey toward financial freedom. Your adventure begins here.

Best wishes on your trading journey.
Much love,
Michael Lamothe
Author of *The Trading Mindwheel*

WHY I WROTE THIS BOOK

Thank you for picking up my book. I know you're busy, so let me get right to it.

This book exists for two reasons:

Reason #1: To provide you with a toolkit to grow wealth and achieve financial freedom.

Reason #2: To help you see immediate improvements in trading and introduce you to my other coaching and services that can help you get better faster.

Using this toolkit to multiply wealth again and again opens up opportunities to live a more satisfying and meaningful life—through both the freedom of financial independence and the time freedom to leave a legacy of service and influence.

This book comes from over thirty years of experience trading, most of it while working 40-60 hours per week as a professional engineer. I'm going to share the good and the bad, the amazing potential and the devastating pitfalls—and maybe a few bubble-bursting truths that other educators might not share.

Sometimes, I'll be blunt. It's all aiming at one target—helping you get better at trading!

While I hope you'll consider using my company's services or hiring me for a more hands-on training experience after reading the methods here, you'll find that my entire trading system is laid out in these pages. There's no extra "secret" after you're done with the book that you'll need for success (other than consistently implementing the knowledge you've gained).

That said, you'll find everything in the book because my overarching goal is to help you. My target is to show you one clear and simple system that works for busy people.

To do that, I structured the book into three parts:

Part One gives you a foundation for the reality of trading. To start, I want you to have a realistic understanding and expectation of what it takes to successfully trade while you're working (or busy with other important things). That way, you'll understand some of the reasons I run my trading system the way I do. It gives a measure of time freedom now, with the potential for financial and ultimate time freedom in the future. There are several self-assessments in this early segment that will also help you understand where you're at and help you determine where you want to be and how to get there. It finishes with a roadmap for how to turn a small nest egg and $100 per month into $1 million in ten years.

In Part Two, you'll learn the meat of the method, as I make the case for a simple trading system that you can automate. This is where I'll teach you the core details of what to trade, when to enter and exit trades, how to execute, how to manage your accounts, and how to handle your own psychology. Automation is why I call my method the AutoPilot

Trading System, but I think you'll be surprised by the other benefits.

Part Three shares the essential steps you can take *now* to put this system to work for your own wealth-building goals. Here's where we break the theory into action steps that you can use to start trading the system on your own. I'll also share some ways that my company can help you get started more quickly, overcome hurdles, and coach you toward mastering the skills and habits necessary to succeed.

It might sound like a lot, but the system is significantly streamlined compared to what you would learn in other trading books. The entire book is about three core ideas:

Idea 1 - You can grow your wealth easier and faster with a clear and simple trading system.

Idea 2 - Mastering a single trade setup will give you more than enough opportunity to grow and compound faster than the indices, especially over the long-term.

Idea 3 - The best way to take advantage of those opportunities is to incorporate that one setup into a complete system. The AutoPilot Trading Method in this book gives you everything you need to start taking those opportunities without letting trading take over your life.

The method you are about to discover greatly simplified my life and my wealth-building efforts. It's helped many of my students to do the same. I hope you'll be able to make the connections for yourself as well, but you'll need to show up ready to learn and willing to shed some old beliefs about trading and wealth.

Most of all, I sincerely hope that you learn how to implement the AutoPilot Trading Method to find freedom for yourself—to grow your wealth with consistency, confidence, and simplicity while you're doing the important work in your career or enjoying retirement.

It's my firm belief that if I can help you build your wealth, it will give you greater confidence and peace of mind in your retirement potential, allowing you to do what you do best. And when you get to a point where you're using that wealth, you can use it not just to live a wonderful life in retirement, but to strengthen your family, support important causes, and maybe even pass on that knowledge to improve the lives of others.

If you read this book and decide you'd like help executing The AutoPilot Trading Method as quickly as possible, you can find out more about our services at AutoPilotTraders.com.

It's my mission to help busy people like you master our trading system so you can build wealth almost on autopilot while you're still working and set you on the path to freedom. And we hope you will be our next great success story.

Buckle up & get ready for takeoff,
Dennis Wilborn

PART ONE

WHY YOU NEED THIS METHOD

CHAPTER ONE

REALITY CHECK

Maybe you've dabbled in trading. Perhaps you tried your hand at day trading or even swing trading. Or you might be one of the brave ones who has waded neck-deep into options trading, forex, or crypto.

My guess is your results weren't what you hoped for. Profits were either inconsistent, or nonexistent, or you had to sacrifice more time and energy than you could afford to earn them. I'm not making this assessment to say that you did anything wrong or that there's anything wrong with you. It's just the nature of the statistics about trading results.

At least 90% of traders lose money, and even more fail to beat the market benchmarks most years. Even among professional money managers, most lag the S&P 500. It's one reason why traditional brokers and money managers insist you can't time the market—because their methods aren't aimed at timing (that, and if more people know how to successfully time the market, it would put money managers out of work).What they're ignoring with their insistence is a long line of successful traders who have used the technical analysis of charts and smart trade management to do just that. Over the last century, numerous high-profile individuals have obliterated the buy and hold myth by trading their way from small stakes to significant wealth, gaining money and time freedom. Many more have done it outside the public eye.

The popular image of those people is usually of the floor-traders at the exchanges, spending all their time and energy flashing fancy hand signals to make instant (and enormous) buy and sell decisions. That makes for great drama, but it's way too stressful for most of us.

However, there is another way. It's a way paved by smart and independent traders since at least the 1920s. One of the most surprising was a professional dancer from Hungary who traded by telegram while traveling the country in the 1950s. As I tell you about the AutoPilot Trading System, you'll see that even he was doing more work than is necessary today.

My Experience Trading on AutoPilot

Let me paint you a quick picture of what life looks like using the AutoPilot Trading Method:

I started beating the S&P every year with this method beginning in 2012. More than that, it hasn't had a losing year since then.

My average return in that period is just over 36%, with some years as high as 70%. At that rate, my actively invested funds have the potential of doubling every two years, according to the classic Rule of 72.

Overall, these results offer me significant peace of mind because of the consistency of profits.

What about the effort required to attain this?

Am I glued to the screen from the opening to the closing bell? Do I have to be right all the time?

No. And No.

I spend about 4 hours per week researching and trading a limited pool of stocks and ETFs for myself and

YEAR	MY LIVE RETURN	S&P 500 RETURN
2012	28.20%	13.41%
2013	44.54%	29.60%
2014	28.16%	11.39%
2015	15.60%	-0.73%
2016	18.81%	9.54%
2017	46.36%	19.42%
2018	36.90%	-6.24%
2019	40.97%	28.88%
2020	69.53%	16.26%
2021	33.00%	26.89%
2022	40.04%	-19.44%

to share with my students. If I were just trading for myself, that would be more like 2 hours per week, maybe less.

My winning rate is about 6 in 10 trades, which means trades are at least a little profitable 60% of the time. Big winners are only a portion of that.

The point is, I love the markets—but they aren't the sole focus of my life!

While I started my investing education as a young pilot in the Navy, I first developed this method when I was working full-time as a professional engineer. I didn't have the luxury of trading during office hours. Fiddling with trading orders at the office weighed on my conscience—and there weren't many hours away from the office. So, I needed something efficient and effective to achieve my trading goals.

Now, I live in Hawaii where the market opens long before dawn. I don't want to wake up when the market opens, watching charts tick away. So, I do a few hours of research on the weekend—including setting up any orders I want to make, or what I'll call trade traps later in this book.

During the week, I do a quick daily check to see if my orders have filled or if I need to make any adjustments because the market has changed. But all my primary decisions are made when the market is closed, so I don't have the emotional confusion of a live chart. It's practically boring compared to the drama of the trading floor. But <u>it's never boring to book consistent profits</u>.

I get even more peace of mind with my Autopilot method of automating orders. This method means I don't have to be watching to know that my capital is protected, and I'll bank profits at the appropriate places.

Most weeks, all this happens without any further action on my part. It can happen while I'm on the road, playing golf, or having breakfast with my wife.

The key to being able to achieve these consistent profits is the AutoPilot Trading Method, the simple one–setup system I'll describe later.

A big part of why it brings me peace of mind, is that it gives me better-than-average market returns, and it only takes a few hours per week.

I proved over a decade ago that I could fit it into a busy schedule. When I was working, I made these trading decisions on weekends and in my spare time. Now that I'm retired, I make my trading decisions around my schedule of running my business, volunteering at my church, mentoring the next generation, playing golf, and spending time with loved ones. That's my idea of freedom. And I'm not the only one with that kind of flexibility.

Member Experiences Trading on AutoPilot

My help is no good if other people can't replicate my experience. Here are some stories from clients about how the AutoPilot Trading Method helped them improve their trading results with more peace of mind:

MARK LANGENBACHER

Mark was a Graham and Buffett style, long-term value investor. However, his results were below his expectations at less than 5% per year.

I think Mark had fair reason to expect he would manage his investments better as a former corporate banker and a professor of economics and finance.

He jumped onboard with me back in 2016, and since then, his results improved dramatically. He's now matching my performance and tells me he averages about 35% per year.

That's over seven times his previous returns, with less effort.

More importantly, he says he's saving hours of research in his trading efforts each week. That's important to him, even now that he's retired, because it gives him the financial freedom to travel, visit family, and continue to build wealth in a way that his fixed retirement plans wouldn't allow.

Here's more of what Mark says in his own words:

> *"If Dennis retired, the processes I learned from him are so strong I could flourish by myself. Dennis does not believe in giving traders fish; he teaches them how to fish!*
>
> *My association with Dennis Wilborn has been life changing. Now I am prepared to trade to supplement my retirement.*
>
> *Thanks to Dennis and his system I will have the money in retirement to travel and visit my far-away family!"*

NICOLE SHIPMAN

Nicole started learning about investing from her father when she was young. He's still an active investor, but his early lessons on value investing led Nicole more toward a buy and hold mentality. During the years that she published her own local magazine, she worked with the value investing and mutual fund approach that she already knew. Then, after selling her business, her interest in the markets blossomed and she decided to become a full-time trader.

She enjoyed buying on pullbacks, just like I teach in the AutoPilot Trading Method. But Nicole struggled with knowing exactly when to exit. She would correctly identify a good buying opportunity and be up 20-50% on a position, but then "round-trip" on a retest of support. Sometimes that meant getting out at breakeven or for a very slight gain.

You can imagine the frustration of watching a double-digit return evaporate.

After joining AutoPilot Trading early in 2023, Nicole says she now understands how the market is working and how things cycle. She's learning how to precisely enter and exit to lock in her gains. She thinks of it as "financing the trade," and with some of our other rules, she's more confident taking larger positions without extra stress.

In her own words, Nicole says:

> *"Dennis is relaxed, even when things go against him. It's helped me with FOMO and to trust in the process and know that you can find stocks and trades at any time. Not being in front of the screen all the time is helpful toward being calm. And it's so relaxing to trade the same things over and over with an attitude that there's always another opportunity.*
>
> *I'm super into this. I just want to get better and better. What I love about trading is that there's always something to learn and improve. You can*

get better and better every day. Dennis' method has made me more com-
mitted and excited to continue on the journey."

ANIL N. PARIKH

I consider Anil to be more of a colleague than a student. He runs an IBD Meetup in Delaware and teaches the Investor's Business Daily method called CANSLIM at the University of Delaware. His experience was good, but he wasn't completely satisfied with his consistency in following his system's rules.

After hearing me speak to Amy Smith on her IBD program years ago, Anil invited me to speak to his Meetup group. Anil isn't specifically using my system, but as a trader who has already mastered his own method, he was able to adapt part of my system to improve his overall results, and that is an honor.

"Long-term, I'm happy to get up to 20% per year," Anil told me. "But because of the parts of AutoPilot Trading that I've incorporated, I'm seeing things get more consistent because of learning from the straightforward approach and discipline."

Anil has been kind enough to join me on some of my weekly live shows and share his own experience and wisdom, so I greatly appreciate his kind words after using just a part of my process to improve his system. It was humbling to me for him to say, "Discipline is the key word for how Dennis has impacted me. My approach and consistency have improved from his influence."

JIM LEE

Jim is an electrical engineer who has been trading for about 6 years. Like a lot of engineers, (myself included) he figured he could take the wealth of free information out there and have no problem figuring out how to trade. When that didn't work, he worked with other mentors or teachers, but hadn't found much success.

He describes his experience as "the typical failing trader. I'd see some success and then have a big drop off." But he didn't want to manage his risk and he'd jump systems as soon as he experienced losses, much like the common trader.

After some self-honesty about his results, Jim found my YouTube channel and gave me a shot because we're both engineers and have similar backgrounds. Since implementing parts of the AutoPilot method, he says he's more consistent and in the green. He's also been overcoming FOMO and finding trading to be simpler and easier to manage while he's still working.

In his own words, he says:

> *"This system has given me more time and lowered my stress. I love that I can do all my orders on the weekend with minimal management during the week. Dennis shows that you don't have to do a lot; just catch part of the moves. There's a calmness about the process that you can trust the process and it'll happen. That's helping me to realize that I won't have to make a killing to retire.*
>
> *Now I can see light at the end of the tunnel. I can see this as a way for me to get my time back instead of sitting at a job all day."*

ROCCO MUSUMECHE

Rocco and I met at church years ago. Rocco is a consummate business professional who is currently building an executive coaching and networking group for CEOs. He knew what I did when we went to church together, but it was years before he showed an interest in learning the system.

"At that point, I just had some investment accounts with a big broker and a financial advisor," Rocco told me. "I didn't know how to read a chart, what a chart looked like, or how to get a chart. It was a mentoring class with Dennis that gave me a foundation to understand how to read charts and really trade. Had I not gone through that training or watched Dennis on the calls and practiced what he taught with paper trading, I still wouldn't know how to trade. But now I have a foundation, and I attribute that all to Dennis."

Because of his extremely busy schedule, Rocco isn't able to devote much time to trading, but even trading a handful of times per year, he's still able to pace the market's average return and keep his skills ready. For the funds he's using to trade, those results are superior to what his financial advisors were able to attain, in his opinion.

"When I look at charts, I can now see those trigger areas all over the chart," he said confidently. "I'm still profiting and know results would improve if I had more time. I'm not looking for 100%. I'm satisfied with the 30-40%."

I could share other stories and messages from people who have improved their returns, used significant gains to pay off student loans, or even buy a dream car, but I think you can see that my method works for people of all sorts.

What's the bottom line?

I'm telling you the stories about my personal experience and the experience of my students to make a point. People who learn and implement the AutoPilot Trading Method grow faster than buy and hold investors—and they usually do it with less stress. Later, we'll explore some buy and hold myths more in-depth, but there should be no argument that averaging 36% per year beats the S&P 500.

It's as simple as this:

- Higher returns = faster growth.
- More frequent high returns = faster compounding.
- Having both elements creates a simpler path to wealth.

What About Options?

If you dig into the numbers, most options investors lose money (just like the 90% figure above). But even for the successful ones—the ones bragging about triple-digit returns online—their overall portfolio returns for the year are commonly in the double digits.

What that means is this: the AutoPilot Trading Method earns you about the same returns as most options investors with far less time invested. Our method is simpler to learn and easier to implement because I designed it to fit my motto: Clarify, Simplify, and Multiply.

The reality is that options require more education and a higher learning curve. Then, you have to spend a lot more time managing trades and evaluating charts. If you want to manage your investments simply, with lower stress, options are NOT the way to go.

On a personal note, I do use options from time to time for certain purposes. I think they can be a useful tool to *layer on top of a successful system or supplement regular trading.* But I would caution against jumping into them before you've mastered simple buying and selling of stocks and ETFs.

I also care a lot about consistency, and options traders can rarely sustain their gargantuan returns from year to year. I'd rather have consistent, moderately high returns than massive swings in my results—even if those big swings are better than the market offers.

Consistency Wins the Race

After reading this book, you will have an effective toolbox with the AutoPilot Trading Method that will allow you to build wealth before you need it. You can learn that method quickly and operate it simply, with minimal time requirements. Even if you are a busy professional, you can secure your retirement and develop wealth far greater than the average investor. Keep reading to find out who this method works best for.

Self-evaluation:

Before jumping to the next chapter, answer the following questions to reveal some of your own beliefs about trading and investing.

1. When it comes to financial decisions, do you?
   - Trust the experts.
   - Go with the crowd.
   - Believe you can make better decisions for your future.

2. In terms of risk, are you?
   - Risk-averse; you'd rather keep most money in cash just in case.
   - Willing to take calculated risks with an acceptable chance of reward.

- A thrill seeker; willing to risk it all for big opportunities.

3. How much experience do you have with trading?
   - This is all new to me.
   - I've dabbled in some investments.
   - I've been trading for a while, and I want to keep improving.

4. How satisfied would you be with an average annual return of 30-40 percent?
   - Ecstatic—it's more than I dreamed possible.
   - Confident: this is a significant and reliable return for growth.
   - Underwhelmed: I need the thrill of 100% plus returns and I want to be rich.

5. How likely are you to regularly commit 2 hours per week to your trading to achieve similar results?
   - Not likely.
   - Moderately likely.
   - Completely committed.

I don't have a scoring or interpretation for your answers to these questions. These questions are intended to get you thinking about your own personality and experience level with financial decisions. Each answer will create its own potential benefits or challenges when it comes to trading live markets, and it's better for you to understand these things about yourself and how they might impact your results.

The question that I believe most impacts your potential to become a great trader is the last one. If you're not going to commit to learning and practicing—even just a little bit each week—you're going to struggle to be consistently profitable...ever. And you can likely kiss any dreams of wealth from this vehicle goodbye.

CHAPTER TWO

WHO THIS BOOK IS FOR

I started trading stocks while working as a naval aviator, and then as a civil engineer. Obviously, in both of those positions, I worked a lot of hours. The investing bug bit me when I was young, much like legendary trader Nicolas Darvas, the Hungarian dancer. When I began to learn more about stocks and technical analysis, I had a dream that I could earn my financial freedom by trading.

The primary challenge in achieving that dream was the long hours I was working. I started reading trading books in my off hours and attending stock trading classes and conferences on the weekends.

Each book and each class gave me new ideas, but because of my inconsistent application I ended up with a hodgepodge trading system that yielded horrible results. I had sacrificed priceless time with my wife and two boys and paid tens of thousands for "training" while facing the shame of a dwindling account on top of it all. In reality, that inconsistency was more from my own pride than my busy schedule.

I'd bought into the marketing promises, let ego fuel my trading decisions, and I lost.

To be completely honest, I even lost money trading for my mother. Not a proud moment.

In hindsight, I now know that I fell into some common traps. Most of them were mistakes in my beliefs and my focus.

Maybe you fell into the same traps.

First, I was tempted by "sexy" strategies. You've probably seen the marketing promises of triple-digit, "can't lose" trades, with the obligatory disclaimer that you probably won't have similar results. Since then, I've learned that sexy strategies feed your ego, not your bottom line.

Second, I was always chasing the next thing: the perfect indicator or the perfect set up. I was looking for the holy grail of trading, the one technique that guarantees amazing returns. I'll tell you now—**it doesn't exist**. The closest thing I found to a holy grail in trading is in my own education and diligence, my consistent application of my rules.

Both of these problems (focus and belief) stemmed from a failure to prioritize the right inputs and outcomes. That failure led to the wrong system for my goals, my abilities, and my lifestyle.

But I never lost faith that trading could be a powerful wealth-builder.

I realized, instead, that I couldn't succeed with those old methods.

I know some other traders have, but it wasn't right for me in my situation. I was already stressed from doing too much at work. Adding the extra stress of making trading choices when I was already tired meant my choices were sub-par from the beginning. The resulting poor trading only led to more stress. You can imagine how this becomes a vicious cycle. A cycle I knew I needed to break.

Since you've read this far, you already know I developed a system that I believe solves these problems. In brief, I'll tell you about the differences between then and now.

First, I spend dramatically less time trading and researching. Streamlining my process and simplifying my decision-making brings down my stress levels and lets me trade with peace of mind. Now, I have more time to do what matters most to me.

You might say, "Dennis, didn't you already tell us that you're not working those long hours anymore?"

Yes, but I developed these strategies while I was still working 10-12-hour days. And I've perfected them while developing my training business and keeping myself busy in my golden years. For me, the old joke is true: I'm busier after "retiring" from the Navy and the corporate world.

Sure, I run a trading education company and trade service now, but I also spend a lot of time having adventures with my wife of almost 50 years, visiting my kids and grandkids on either side of the Pacific Ocean, mentoring younger married couples, and serving on the board of a non-profit. All of which gives me good reasons to keep my trading process short!

The second massive shift is that I simplified my trading decisions. My problems were problems of focus and beliefs. So, the solution had to address both.

First, I let go of needing to know and do everything. I realized I only had time to deal with a handful of stocks, so I went through a prolonged process of whittling down how many tickers I was paying attention to. In hindsight, I probably should have narrowed my focus further and sooner. On the other side of that choice, I now see that watching fewer stocks allows me to know and understand how they move better while reducing my time in research.

In addition to reducing the number of entities, I reduced the number of potential entry and exit triggers I would trade. But I didn't just pick the ones I liked. <u>I analyzed past market behavior to find the ones that were most common and most powerful</u>. That way, I knew I was looking at the best prospective trades each week.

Another way that I simplified my trading decisions was to develop checklists like those I used as a pilot. The checklists helped remove emotions and made it easier to stay on task.

The result: <u>more consistent profits and growth with less time invested</u>. As I mentioned before, consistency allows me to take better advantage of compounding. If your returns experience wild swings, i.e., being up 50% one year and down 40% the next, compounding does not have the repetition it needs to grow wealth.

Consistency allows even small profits to grow into large amounts. Just look at Warren Buffett, who secured an average return of about 20% from 1965 to 2020. If we can hone our practice so that we can get large profits consistently, it's easier to see how we can then grow wealth rapidly.

Two changes had the biggest effect on my efforts.

First, I tailored my training. That is, I clarified my purpose and goals so that everything lined up.

What that meant in practice is that I cherry-picked the best strategies of the systems that I had spent decades learning, and pulled what worked for me into an efficient system. That clarity allowed me to focus on what mattered, and I got to know my trade process and setups very, very well. I didn't need to guess if a trade was right because I had factual evidence to tell me when to pull the trigger. On the back end, I had automated processes that protected capital and secured profits.

Second, I narrowed my focus. I simplified everything. From a smaller batch of stocks to chasing fewer signals, I streamlined rigorously. That simplicity eliminated confusion and subjectivity. The urge to trade impulsively slowly died as I found that a simple, disciplined approach earned me the profits I desired.

Together, clarifying and simplifying my system is what led to multiplying my profits. It also offered the freedom to grow my wealth in a systematic way that still allowed me to live my life. That's how, "Clarify. Simplify. Multiply," became my motto.

If that sounds appealing to you, keep reading and we'll look at all the pieces of the AutoPilot Trading Method together.

Let's start by defining goals.

To begin, let's figure out some benchmark goals and define a successful system for a busy professional. This process is as much about you as it is about the market, because your life isn't all about the money.

Even if it were, you would have unique constraints on your time. Ability must also be considered as you develop your trading system. The AutoPilot Trading Method we're going to lay out works, so we recommend focusing on and learning a good system like this one before doing any tweaks to try to make it better. As an engineer, I understand the urge. Hold off.

Here are the basic elements of a successful system like the AutoPilot Trading Method:
- Simple to learn: clarity of action.
- Simple to do: consistency of action.

- Works while you work: time efficiency & automation.
- Repeated market patterns & behaviors: recurring opportunities.
- Puts your money to work: capital deployment.
- Avoids unnecessary risk: capital preservation.
- Prioritizes compounding: feeds the wealth plan.
- Beats the market: increases the speed of compounding.

Many think a system needs many parts to do so much. My results are proof they don't. Mastering one setup and the proper management is enough.

Most traders fail and quit because the education they receive is too complicated to learn or implement. Without enough experience to gain confidence, it's easier to go back to buy and hold, or let a professional manage your future.

What about metrics? Pulling from one of the classic books on trend trading, *Trend Trading for A Living* by Dr. Thomas Carr, **a 40% annual return is a reasonable goal for most trend trading systems**. We have twelve years of experience to vouch for this as a benchmark, having earned just over 36% per year on average. Some years will be higher, some lower. But we hope to avoid the traditionally expected volatility in trend trading systems, where some years you're up 50%, followed by a year of 20% losses. Many trend traders are willing to accept up to 30% account drawdowns before they see a problem with the system! [1]

The other important metric is the Win:Loss ratio. Simply put, how many of your trades are profitable and how many are not? I believe a reasonable ratio is 60:40; that is out of 100 trades, 60 are winners and 40 are losers. With proper

---

[1] See *The Way of the Turtle* by Curtis M. Faith. McGraw Hill, 2007, Pg. 87

money management and risk management, this ratio is adequate to achieve our profit goals. My personal goal, however, is 65/35.

|+◇|◇

To finally answer the question at the top of this chapter, this book is for you if:

- You want to learn how to grow wealth through trading.
- You're busy, and you don't have time to waste on learning or implementation.
- You want clear and simple trading decisions.
- You're comfortable taking small, defined risks for the opportunity of reasonable profits.
- You're committed to consistently following a proven system.
- You agree that 30-40% average annual returns are an adequate goal for wealth-building.
- You agree that 2-3 hours per week is a reasonable commitment to achieve such returns.

If that sounds like you, the next chapter will expose some of the myths surrounding the markets that even the most ambitious new traders have to overcome to find success.

Self-evaluation:

Answer the following questions and rate yourself on how well your current trading system or past trading system delivers on the core metrics and basic elements of a successful system.

- Is the system easy to learn?
- Is the system easy to manage on a daily or weekly basis?
- Does it include any automation or time-saving elements?
- Is it based on repeated market patterns that provide enough opportunity?
- Alternatively, are there so many setups or triggers that it's hard to choose the "right" one?
- Is your capital working consistently?
- Does it avoid unnecessary risks?
- How frequently do profits come in that can be reinvested?
- Does it consistently beat the market?
- Does the system have an expected return of about 30-40%?
- What is the Win:Loss ratio?

Spend the time to answer these questions, even if it takes a bit of research or accounting. At best, you'll be more confident in your system. Or you might realize that you've been trading with a significant handicap—and this book can help you repair it.

CHAPTER THREE

THE BIG LIES OF NORMAL TRADING

Wall Street, financial news, money managers, and retirement planners all tout some form of buy and hold as the best method for investing. In some sense, it's the consensus of the experts that investing little amounts consistently into the market and leaving that money there is the best secret to big returns.

I'm a contrarian; I disagree. I have four primary reasons:

1. Lack of control. If I stick my money in the market and leave it there, I have to take what the market gives me. Good or bad; profits or losses. They claim that leaving your money with them and letting the market do its thing works over the long-term. But in reality, people experience a lot of stress and anguish when their 401(k) gets cut in half in short order. It happened in 2001, again in 2008, and a third time in 2020. The reasons don't matter so much as the experience. If you don't take control, you're along for the ride. And if your retirement date winds you up in one of the troughs, your golden years might look more like bronze years.

2. Lackluster returns. Repeated roller coaster plunges aside, the experts tout investing for the long-term as the solution. If you look at long-term averages, the S&P returns about 10% percent per year from 1965 to 2020 [2], as calculated by Berkshire Hathaway. That includes dividends reinvested, and that number holds up over the long-term, although a 10 or 20-year period can vary dramatically. [3] It must be said that almost nobody in the professional money management space even matches those returns regularly, because they don't plan for it. None of the pros at the brokerage houses recommend putting your money 100% into a benchmark like the S&P 500 ETF. So, the benchmark returns they often tout don't line up with the reality of how anybody invests! It's just a measuring stick. In reality, the average money manager plans for returns as low as 6.6% nearing retirement according to the Motley Fool. And the average retail investor does as little as 4.25% per year according to research from Dalbar, Inc. [4] Throw in inflation, taxes, account fees, and you're sitting on the slow boat to wealth generation. I don't have a hundred years to compound gains. I want more now.

3. One-size-fits-all results. Using a benchmark as the assumption for calculating returns and retirement growth leads to poor predictive results. As mentioned above, if your retirement year lands in a trough or a downturn, your nest egg isn't going to

2. https://www.berkshirehathaway.com/letters/2020ltr.pdf

3. For the 20 years ending 12/31/19, the average was only 6.06%

4. https://wealthwatchadvisors.com/wp-content/up-loads/2020/03/QAIB_PremiumEdition2020_WWA.pdf

provide nearly as much retirement income as you hoped for. There are ways to counter that, but the buy and hold crowd claims there's too much risk to do so. If you are lucky enough to retire during a market peak, and remove all of your funds from the market, your retirement manager looks like a genius. Personally, I don't want my investments to have that much chance involved when *a little attention and effort on my part can earn me consistent growth even after I retire.*

4. Roller coaster experiences. I don't know about you, but I don't like losing. I especially don't like that gut churning feeling of opening my accounts to discover that my money has dwindled away with a market drop while I sat by and did nothing. A couple of easy risk management practices can get rid of most roller-coaster experiences, meaning your losses become smaller and your gains grow.

Now that we've covered the problems with the conventional model, let's turn our attention to the typical advice on actively trading that we see in most books and courses.

$$| +\phi + \phi$$

If you've spent any time at all learning to trade, you recognize how quickly this turns into a complicated endeavor. Let's break down the most common issues with many professional trading systems.

5. Too big a universe of stocks. I have known traders who try to watch hundreds of stocks daily. They never last long with that practice. Even if they did, narrowing down your decision parameters allows you to focus on the best opportunities. Watching too

many stocks encourages decision fatigue and burn-out, as well as averaging down potential returns.

6. Too many moving parts. Between chart styles, price signals, indicators, price patterns, candlestick patterns, volume, and several other primary, secondary, and tertiary tools for analyzing and predicting trades, most systems simply have too many parts. Busy professionals who also want to trade already have to make too many decisions. I've seen many students get bogged down in finding a trigger, talking themselves into or out of a trade, and then beating themselves up when things don't work out the way they hoped. That's why the AutoPilot Trading Method focuses on a single three-step trade setup. One choice, simple decisions, better profits.

7. Too much to learn before you start. Some very successful but traditional systems require wading through very thick volumes filled with charts and data to learn how to trade. Some focus on complex interactions of economic indicators and individual stock factors just to narrow down your list of potential trades. Then, you have to learn all the ways you can enter and exit the trade. Complexity leads to confusion, which leads to bad results. I've been there; I know the ups and downs associated with complex decisions on investments. I prefer a simple, visual indication that it's time to buy or sell. I also prefer a single-setup system with a short set of rules so I can get started quickly. Even if I start with practice (paper trading), I can grow my wealth sooner with a simple, winning system than with a more complex system.

8. Too many setups or triggers. Just as with trimming down your watchlist, having multiple potential set-ups or triggers that you're looking for breeds confusion. If I have fifty stocks I'm watching and twelve of them provide potential setups on eight different chart patterns, how do I decide which one is best? Which one has the most potential for profit? Which one is the least risky? How do I test to get data on these questions efficiently if I'm looking at so many different pieces? With a simpler system, I can learn faster, test faster, and implement faster.

9. Combining the previous four problems, we end up with the big daddy problem of complexity. Under most systems, trading becomes an extra job. A job that requires intense time researching, evaluating, and analyzing—then deciding and implementing. Complexity makes it harder to learn, harder to implement, and harder to track. I know some traders who work over forty hours per week in their profession and then work 20 to 40 extra hours watching the market. I tried it myself for a while, and it nearly drove me into the ground. Set yourself up for success by ditching the extra baggage.

As you'll learn in this book, it doesn't have to be this way.

|ₜ🮂🮂

Survey after survey shows that over 90% of traders lose money, especially day traders. Some even say only 1% become consistently profitable. Among professional money managers, about 85% underperform their benchmarks over time. [5] Most of the famous traders who became successful blew up at least one account along the way.

The truth is, trading ain't easy!

It takes work and diligence—consistently applied. There could be many reasons why the stats hold true year-to-year, but the only conclusion you hear from the financial media is typically this: "trading can be hazardous to your wealth." Their prescription is to buy and hold, use asset allocation, trust the averages, and hope you retire during a boom cycle.

As a contrarian, I think there are other possible conclusions and prescriptions. I'm led to ask: if other people have had success, what did they have in common? Is there a sweet spot between buy and hold, and trading so much that it hinders your results?

Here are some of the challenges of trading I think we have solutions for:

1. Confusion born of complexity. I've already dealt with the complexity question, and how it leads to confusion in trading decisions. Eliminate the complexity and you get clarity. This alone would change most traders' experience of dealing with the market—and it's why I ruthlessly simplified.

2. The ticker trap. Many traders, new and old, get sucked into watching every price change. Watching the ticker increases emotions. Increased emotions lead to erratic decision-making. Even those traders who have a solid system that they've practiced can talk themselves into poor, impulsive decisions when

---

5. https://www.cnbc.com/2020/11/20/attention-robinhood-power-users-most-day-traders-lose-money.html

they're watching the ticks. Impulsive trading takes out many good technicians. It's one reason I set my system on AutoPilot!

3. Trading strategies without a system. This problem is most consistent with newbies trying to learn how to trade. It's probably most common in times of market peaks—when everyone thinks they can't lose. During the 2000 dot com bubble, people began throwing money into the stock market because it always went up. The same phenomenon happened in the housing bubble, where people overleveraged themselves to get into houses that would "never go down in value." But as in life, gravity is a force in markets. Buying because of market hype leads to selling during market panic. Buying because of a hot tip leads to poor, inconsistent results, or outright scams. Buying the no-lose options strategy without understanding when and how to use it led to the biggest losses I've seen among friends and students. A system gives you guide rails to keep you on track. A system simplifies decisions by letting you make them apart from the emotions of the market. This book gives you a complete system and strategies to reduce those emotions.

4. Discipline. Even traders who have a system are constantly tempted to break the rules. The call of the easy path is always strong, and it's easier to hand your money to a money manager and accept average returns than it is to make your own choices and take your own risks. It's easier to watch TV instead of doing market research. Without discipline, results lag. It's simply human nature: If we want to engage in discipline, it's much easier with a simple system.

Part of my discipline includes habits and routines that reinforce discipline.

5. Psychology. The ups and downs of the market can mess with your brain and your emotions. Entire books have been written (and I recommend reading them) about how easily we can fool ourselves into bad decision-making. With a system and discipline, psychology can be tamed. But it's the head game that takes out most potential traders. I'll cover some psychology within this book, but my preferred strategy is to change how you play the game so that you're less likely to experience those troubles. You can find my list at AutoPilotTraders.com/ReadingList.

6. Compounding. One of my favorite books about money is also one of the simplest. *The Richest Man in Babylon* by George S Clayson presents a simple roadmap for money management, investing, and wealth-building. Through the story of an ancient scribe turned moneylender, we learn that the two simple keys to wealth are self-discipline and the principle of compounding. Get your money working for you, and then keep engaging those returns.

In teaching compounding, the mentor of the story says, "Don't eat the children of your savings." Many traders gain some level of success and begin spending their profits. While there is a time and place for rewarding yourself for good work, be careful that you don't derail your compounding train. Forgetting that compounding is always at work robs you of potential returns you could have gained if you had been more purposeful. I would have significantly more wealth today if I had learned this earlier.

It's a bit easier when your money is parked in a retirement account to not spend it. But you still need the intentional effort to grow it.

Compounding is not a mystical phenomenon that magically turns little things into big things. It's simply the multiplied effect of little actions over time.

With discipline and planning, we can use compounding strategically to reach our goals sooner by working to increase returns. Or we can dial it back for a more relaxed approach.

Compounding is the true secret to attaining wealth, not just securing retirement.

The AutoPilot Trading method aims at managing or eliminating all of the things that can get in the way of compounding returns—and most traders find that they are the biggest thing getting in the way.

Once you get your system and mentality lined up, you'll be surprised at what's possible and how easy successful trading can be.

$$|_+\Phi|\bar{\varphi}$$

Self-evaluation:

Answer the following questions and rate yourself on how well you understand the primary problems and how many of them you believe.

First, rate your system on how well it handles the primary problems covered. 1 is low and 5 is high.

Does your system deliver a few good candidates (1), or large lists of stocks to trade (5)?

Does your system work with a few moving parts (1), or does it have many overlapping layers of analysis and research to consider every week (5)?

Can your system be understood and learned in a few days (1), or will it take months/years of study (5)?

Does your system have one or two setups/triggers (1) or many (5)?

Can trading decisions be made by answering a handful of fact-based questions on a single page (1), or does it require consulting a mix of potentially conflicting signals (5)?

Does your system rely on observable and objective chart information (1), or does it rest on tips, hunches, or guesses (5)?

The higher the overall score (closer to 30), the less consistent the system will be and the more difficult it will be to use.

Now, rate yourself on trading habits from 1-5.

How often are you uncertain or confused about whether a signal has a high potential for success?
Almost never (1) - Most of the time (5)

How common is it for you to find yourself watching the ticker to see what happens, and whether your trading decisions pan out?
Almost never (1) - Most of the time (5)

How often do you trade a strategy without a complete understanding of how it affects your trading system?

Almost never (1) - Most of the time (5)

Do you struggle with making trading a priority?

Almost never (1) - Most of the time (5)

Do you ever experience extreme emotional swings due to trading?

Almost never (1) - Most of the time (5)

A low score means you are on track and implementing the Autopilot Trading System should be relatively simple for you.

A high score (closer to 25) means you might have some bad habits to overcome, but also that dedication to a system like Autopilot Trading will have the most positive impact on your results.

CHAPTER FOUR

WHY THIS METHOD WORKS

I think it's appropriate to have a healthy skepticism about systems or programs that promise big results. When even professional money managers think that it's impossible to time the market, it's understandable why most people think that trading systems are something of a pipe dream.

We've already shared with you some of the results we've enjoyed with the system for the last 11 years. You've heard stories from some of my students about their successes— some even beat me with a bit more work.

Now, let me briefly share with you the reasons why the AutoPilot Trading Method achieves consistent returns, even against the apparent odds.

First, the system was designed for simplicity. Simplicity helps manage the problems of complexity and inconsistency in results. And like I said above, simplicity makes it easier to implement and remain disciplined.

Further, the AutoPilot Trading Method has some flexibility in implementation, making it easy to integrate into your life. If you're strapped for time, just fall back on some basics to continue getting good results with even less time. When you're ready to ramp up the returns, you can incrementally increase your effort to get better results.

The method also focuses on objective **Value Action Zones**. That is, a handful of visual clues on the chart show us a trade is setting up in a certain area. I purposefully chose the visual cues that are hard to confuse or misinterpret. Then, when the clues are clear, we determine measured, evidence-based points where we want to act!

Catching great trades in this way can be a bit like setting traps. If our trade order is like a mousetrap, we determine where to set it by looking at the clues that a mouse has snuck into our house (holes, chewed up food, droppings). Evaluating those clues gives you factual proof that a mouse has been there. Set traps where those clues are strongest, and many of them will work. Then you can sleep easier knowing you don't have a mouse anymore…or that your trades are catching profits instead of losses.

Our **Value Action Zones (VAZs)** give us a good opportunity for success in any one trade. And as you'll hear from me often, "it doesn't happen every time, but it does happen all the time." Our job as traders is to trust the system and set up profit traps.

⊦₊φ⊦ϙ

Along with simplicity, the AutoPilot Trading Method offers more control. Buy and hold investors experience both the roller coaster ride of market cycles, and the crapshoot of what the market is doing when they decide to retire. Trading smart lets you choose the most profitable times to ride the roller coaster rather than being taken for a ride.

What do I mean by that? Learning a simple system gives you the tools to decide when you're invested and when you're not. You can be in for the ride up, but hold onto your profits when the market falls.

Or, with a little more work and a couple of lesser-known tools, you can profit when the market falls as well. It's not our preferred play, but it is an option for those willing to learn another discipline.

⊦₊╬⊦╬

As part of the AutoPilot Trading Method, we'll also teach you our concept of "Strategic Compounding". In a nutshell, when you can make decent returns more frequently, those numerous opportunities give you the advantage of compounding returns faster. Like our mousetrap example above, the sooner you refresh successful traps, the more mice you catch.

It's simple math. But doing your math on the front end helps you gauge decisions about your trading. Rather than exploring the math on the backend to learn how you've done in hindsight, we want you to be purposeful about your returns. Planning our compounding efforts ahead of time gives us both more control and more peace of mind.

⊦₊╬⊦╬

Time is the fourth benefit of the AutoPilot Trading Method. While traditional trading systems are complex and take a long time to learn—let alone a long time to master— you can learn the AutoPilot Trading Method in a weekend.

Once you've learned it, you control how much time you decide to spend implementing it. For some students, a little extra time invested reaps large increases in their returns, but personally, I'd rather earn a healthy return (close to 40%) and spend my days doing other meaningful things. In this area, the AutoPilot Trading Method excels at customization. My most time-strapped students may limit their trades to just a few times a year and still equal or beat the market averages, while enjoying the control and peace of mind avoiding the rollercoaster.

To eliminate a couple of our complaints about traditional methods of trading, we've added automation to the AutoPilot Trading Method.

Automating the most volatile part of any trading system automatically gives you a higher probability of consistency and success, reduces the stress of making decisions, and increases your sense of comfort and peace of mind. We'll get more into the methods and practices of automating the system later, but this one tool of the AutoPilot Trading Method can be plugged into other trading systems if you decide to go a different route.

In summary, I designed the AutoPilot Trading Method to address the specific problems detailed in the last chapter— the same ones I experienced while learning to trade and holding down a professional job. If you spend the time to learn the method and enact the plan with focus, you can enjoy the same benefits.

Self-Review:

Answer the questions in the self-evaluation below to see how your trading efforts stack up on these parameters.

- Does your current system give you observable and objective areas to act?

- Are you in control of your decisions with your current methods, and do they reduce impulsiveness?
- Does your system allow for flexible implementation that fits into your schedule, or do you need to be watching the market all the time?
- Is your current method adjustable for different market conditions or flexible for seasons in your life when you might have more or less time to trade?
- Can your current trading plan be used to map out a financial road to success?
- Does your system allow you to automate every trade action?

CHAPTER FIVE

WHO THIS ISN'T FOR

If you've read this far, I hope you see the potential in the AutoPilot Trading Method. But I want to be realistic and recognize that this method isn't for everyone. So, let me share a few things that might make this method more challenging, or unworkable for you.

Unrealistic Expectations

If you're hoping that this method will turn five hundred dollars into five million within a year, it's not for you. This is *not* a get-rich-quick scheme, or a path to instant wealth. And I firmly believe some old words of wisdom that "wealth quickly gained is soon lost" [6].

If you follow the AutoPilot Trading Method, you have the potential to amass significant wealth—and then use that to attain financial freedom, but a slew of factors will affect how quickly and how easily you achieve that goal. If you come to this method ready to learn and put in your own work, the AutoPilot Trading Method will give you a clear path.

---

[6] Proverbs 13:11

A healthy attitude about money will go a long way toward your success as well.

Relentless Tinkering

I'm an engineer, I get it; there's always a temptation to tweak and fiddle, to find the most optimized version of a system. Heck, as some of my student success stories show, there are increased gains to be had with my own system if you're willing to put in extra time and effort. But, imagine what it would be like to board an aircraft and then see the pilot outside your window, tinkering with the wings…

After over 30 years of trading, I've learned the hard way to find something simple that works and be satisfied with exceptional results. What's the point of shockingly high gains if you drive yourself into the ground to get them?

To paraphrase other old words of wisdom: what's the point if you gain the world but lose your soul?

If you are prone to always trying to reinvent the wheel or tweaking something outside of the scope of its parameters, this may not work for you.

If you are ready to learn a system that is proven and master it, then you can earn much better than market returns with minimal strain.

Once you have one working system mastered, then you have the liberty of choosing to add other elements or to pursue other systems if you think they can improve your returns. But master one good system first, so you always have a fallback.

I've known too many traders (and been guilty of it myself) who dabble in multiple systems and never become proficient in one. The results speak for themselves: inconsistency, losing money, or giving up on trading and the related dreams.

The successful traders I have met or studied became masters of their method. You can't escape this necessity.

Commit to mastery, and you'll have unimaginable potential.

Poor Discipline (or an entitlement mindset)

A certain level of mental toughness and resiliency separates successful traders from hobbyists. We have already talked about the need for discipline, so that is one aspect of mindset that you need to bring to the table. But mastering any trading system is easier when you have a good grasp on your own strengths and weaknesses, including, or especially, your propensity for impulsiveness and emotional decision-making.

If you haven't already done this work, you might struggle with the system—or any system. At the very least, come willing to observe and learn these things about yourself. I firmly believe that traders are made, not born, but our personalities and character traits can help or hinder us.

Most of the skills and habits can be learned and honed if you're willing to do the work.

However, if you think the market owes you something, trading may not be right for you, regardless of the system you choose.

The most successful traders I know are adapters; solution-oriented, accepting responsibility for their decisions and actions, and tailoring solutions to their own situation (once mastery is accomplished).

Pride and Thrill-Seeking

There's an old saying, "Pride goes before a fall." It's a little more of that old wisdom I take to heart in life and trading. Pride is one of two character defaults that can ruin a trading account and a whole lot else.

Pride tends to get traders focused on being right. Even when a trade goes against them, as happens sometimes, they will insist that their set up was proper and that things should go their way. This clouds decision-making and compounds losses.

When you don't want to admit the trade went against you, you might double down or write it off and lose more than you can afford. If you hold on as the thing tanks, you might justify your decision or bargain with yourself about silly ideas like getting out when you're back to breakeven.

This sets you up for more impulsive decision-making on the next trade. But being humble enough to admit the trade didn't work out allows you to be clearheaded and make good decisions both with the current position, and for the next opportunity.

Risk seeking or adrenaline chasing is the other character defect that can hammer away at your accounts. If you feel compelled to take a trade, any trade, you might be suffering from this. If you only count the potential profit of the setup and don't weigh the potential risk, you might also be suffering from this.

The way to overcome it is patiently waiting for those clues that tell you it's time to set a trap. Stepping away from trading for a short time can also be helpful in this case.

Obviously, any trading involves a level of risk, so the decision to invest means you probably have a level of risk tolerance. But serious and professional traders take calculated, smart risks, not random, undefined risks.

For success, trade on purpose, according to your plan. Keep your emotions out of the process and let the outcome inform you.

Unwillingness to Learn and Grow

We all tend to have our ways of doing things. It's human. If you're coming to this book with an established set of trading habits, maybe you're looking for the trick or tip that will make the difference for you. In that case, I'm sure you'll find some helpful ideas in these pages, but you may not get all the benefits of the entire system if you approach it that way. Consider learning the thing as a complete system and compare it to others.

Even if you are new to trading, you might need to jettison some previous beliefs about money or the stock market to find the most success. Trading is a skill, and each system entails a particular skill set. If it gets into your head, but you've never practiced it, you're going to struggle to be successful. Learning, in this case, means putting the theory into practice and struggling through the learning curve until you reach mastery. That's where growth comes in.

If you aren't ready to approach learning the system with that mindset, it may not be for you.

Insufficient Capital

If you are starting off with a smaller capital pool, it will grow more slowly in the beginning. But you will need at least a small amount of savings to invest, and it's wise to continue committing to your future by contributing regularly—even if that amount is small. Just make sure the money you're investing is truly the extra that's available after meeting your basic needs right now. If you need help mastering basic budgeting, then you're not quite ready to tackle investing. You first need a foundation. Get financially healthy first, then you can work on getting financially fit.

We'll cover the specifics of the roadmap to $1M, including a recommendation on minimum capital in the next chapter.

People with access to larger savings or retirement accounts may not feel the urgency of continuing to contribute if you are gaining large returns. I think that's a mistake, and endangers your focus and commitment to your future. Progress is easier to make with small, regular strides than in giant leaps.

And you'll be amazed what those small seeds of investment turn into after a few cycles of compounding.

In all cases, you should never trade with money you can't afford to lose! If you bet the farm, you might end up homeless. Some traders have recovered from that. Most don't.

These Traits Lead to Success

In my experience coaching others, these traits are the most helpful in creating a solid trader:
- Commitment to Mastery
- Humble enough to learn at a deep level
- Adaptable within a sound framework
- Dedication to self-improvement and discipline
- Self-awareness of your risk tolerances, motivations, strengths, and weaknesses.

Potential Downsides

One final note on this topic, there are some potential downsides to the AutoPilot Trading Method for some people. However, they're basically the same downsides as any other system.

You will sometimes miss out on potential trade opportunities.

Of course, that would be true of any trading method unless you have unlimited funds and time to deploy them. In this case, it's part of the design. In my system, we limit the number of trades we're actively managing, so that we don't get overwhelmed. That means you might see opportunities while you're fully invested. And the beauty is, you shouldn't need to worry about it because your profits will likely be working out nicely. If you want more practice to hone your skills, you can always use those opportunities to paper trade.

You will have some winners and some losers.

Again, this is common to all trading systems. If you aren't ready to accept this truth, then trading itself may not be right for you. The question is what ratio of winners to losers you are willing to accept. I've already defined my target ratio as 60/40. I'll get into the exact math of that later in the book, but it's a commonly accepted expectation for trend trading systems or swing trading ones like the AutoPilot Trading Method.

There's a level of patience and control required.

Again, this is part of the design. So if you struggle with being patient, you can work on that as part of your discipline, or perhaps find a more suitable trading system for your style. As for control, actively managing a portfolio is what allows me and my students to achieve higher than average returns consistently. Bucking against that may mean trading isn't your best path to investing.

Slow and steady versus explosive growth.

Some folks who may not exactly be the egotistic, thrill-seeker type might still prefer the intrigue and the bragging rights that come from explosive growth by trading options or more aggressive stock systems. I've already addressed what I see as the weaknesses and inconsistencies of this type of approach versus the consistent and purposeful growth of a slow and steady model like the AutoPilot Trading Method. Of course, my slow and steady knocks the socks off traditional buy and hold expectations.

Again, it comes down to personal preference. If you don't like the idea of 40% per year as a repeated target and would prefer to find a system that offers more volatile returns, knock yourself out. You can find systems that offer 100-200%+ returns in a good year, but suffer 50% losses in a bad year. You're free to learn them instead. My feelings won't be hurt. I took that same road for a time.

But now, I stick with the AutoPilot Trading Method because it solves some of the problems I already addressed. And I'm comfortable knowing that the people who agree with my philosophy are going to profit handsomely.

Self-Evaluation:

Take the survey below to check your own readiness for the AutoPilot Trading Method. Consider journaling about these questions to get deep about your own potential for success with the Autopilot System or trading in general.

Do you believe your expectations are realistic for the potential benefits and risks of trading?

- Are you willing to follow a system until you have made it work, or are you a tinkerer?
- How strong are you at creating and maintaining habits - otherwise known as self-discipline?
- Do you need to be right or can you honestly evaluate when you've made mistakes and course-correct?
- Do you need the adrenaline of risk or can you act systematically?
- How willing are you to learn and grow? Try to think of some examples from your past.
- Is there a pool of capital that you can afford to risk as you learn?
- Would you say you have most of the character traits that aid in success? (Pages 46)
- Are you willing to accept the downsides of trading a system?

PART TWO

THE ROADMAP

CHAPTER SIX

HOW TO TURN $100 PER MONTH INTO $1 MILLION IN 10 YEARS

We are finally here at the roadmap to Trade Your Way to Freedom. Every journey begins somewhere, and as we start ours, we begin with the understanding that most of our path comes down to math problems.

I'm going to start with some basic assumptions to get where we want to go. Your circumstances will probably differ, which might make it easier or harder for you to reach that first big milestone. But the basics will hold, and you can plug your own numbers in to create a customized roadmap.

Here are the data points to fill out the roadmap, customize it to your situation, and adjust it to keep yourself on track.

- A starting point
- Target rate of return
- Regular contributions
- Time

This is probably the most complex math we have in this book, which is why we suggest you use a calculator like this one. https://www.thecalculatorsite.com/finance/calculators/compoundinterestcalculator.php

Our assumptions are:
- Starting point = $18,000
- Rate of return = 40% per year compounded monthly
- Monthly contributions = $100
- Time = 10 years

If you care to do it longhand, the formula is:

$$FV = P\left(1+\frac{i}{c}\right)^{n \times c} + \frac{R\left(\left(1+\frac{i}{c}\right)^{n \times c} - 1\right)}{\frac{i}{c}}$$

FV = Future Value
P = Principal
i = Annual Interest Rate
c = Compounding Frequency
n = Number of Years
R = Amount of Monthly Contribution

You can get a full breakdown of the formula at https://www.wikihow.com/Calculate-Compound-Interest

Otherwise, plugging those 4 data points into a compounding calculator gives us a ten-year account value of $1,071,167.45, easily reaching our $1M goal. Our total contributions over the life of our plan are just $30,000 ($18,000 + 120 months of $100 contributions). This shows you how important high returns and compounding are. You can speed things up by starting with or contributing greater amounts.

This is largely a conceptual framework that you can use to set your targets simply and easily. Think of each data point like a puzzle piece. Want to change the destination? Plug in a different number and see how that affects your path. Now, let's briefly cover each point.

A starting point: Some nest egg or initial account value that you've accumulated. The starting point for our example roadmap is an initial account size of $18,000.

Based on US survey numbers about retirement savings, this is fairly common for people in their peak earning years at all income levels. If you're a well-paid professional, it shouldn't be out of the question. Again, you may have more or less, but that's not the important thing.

Your starting point doesn't determine your ultimate destination. Your discipline and execution get you there. I've known great traders who start with only $5,000. That just comes with different challenges.

When it comes to your success, you bring more to the table than anything else!

Target rate of return: Our system target is 40%. As of this writing, we are on track to have another year of around 40% in 2023, bringing our ten-year average to a bit over 36.84% if we stay the course.

Even though I had years of experience trading before implementing this system, I also had a learning curve to trade the system well in the early years—though we still beat the S&P every year, with no losing years. Still, those early years weigh down my overall average. But good execution in later years has brought it back within striking distance of my target goal.

The target is a target. Sometimes, you hit it; sometimes, you go over or under. The point is to keep aiming for consistency. Using 40% puts you in line with most trend trading systems and among great professional traders.

Regular contributions: Adding funds is important for a couple of reasons. If your starting account is small, you may want to add more funds to catch up, giving you the ability to start compounding more rapidly. If you're starting with our example ($18,000) or more, adding funds is about staying in the game. It's about keeping yourself engaged in your education and your investments.

For our example, one hundred dollars per month is not a huge investment, and it is not the main driver of our compounding. Don't get me wrong, adding those small amounts regularly adds up over time. But with a large rate of return like 40%, that's what's driving our compounding. The contributions are part of our mindset. It helps us focus on the fact that these are hard-earned dollars we are investing, and we need to treat them with that significance.

Each contribution is a representation of the hours we spent earning that money. When we invest it, our aim is to multiply those dollars so that we have more hours in the future for something better than simply earning a living.

Again, our roadmap is something that you fill in with your numbers. If you have exactly $18,000, you can work to follow our plan, but you're probably going to have a different starting amount. If you are in the US, you can most definitely add one hundred dollars per month by adjusting a few priorities. If you absolutely cannot commit to that, you may need to consult other books about getting your finances in order before taking up trading. Please don't squander your future by overspending today. With a roadmap like this, diligently followed, you can have anything you want with some patience. And you'll enjoy the excitement of watching your account grow each month and each year.

Tracking all of that is something we'll discuss toward the end of the book. So, for now, I'll just mention that you should plan to keep good records and do a regular review of your results to help you stay on track.

The key to growing a small amount into a large amount in a relatively short time (ten years is comfortable) is the rate of return.

The rest of this book is focused on the method we use to earn our target rate. Without that, in the world of average stock returns, we'd be looking at decades to achieve the same goal. That's exactly what money managers and invest-ment advisors preach.

Self-Evaluation:

Keep reading to discover our simple method for earning such a high rate of return consistently. But first, use this cal-culator to customize your roadmap, and answer a few questions below to get yourself started on this journey.
https://www.thecalculatorsite.com/finance/calcula-tors/compoundinterestcalculator.php

What are your numbers for the 4 data points?

How does our target rate of return change your potential time to retirement or your wealth accumulation goal?

Write out some short-term and long-term goals that break down the big goal into smaller pieces.

Rate your commitment level to following your path.

Why do you want to accomplish these goals?

What will motivate you to stay on track and overcome challenges?

I'd recommend keeping your roadmap in a place where you can review it regularly, evaluate your progress, and adjust as needed. I like to have it at the front of my trade journal that I use every week.

CHAPTER SEVEN

THE 6 PILLARS OF ANY SUCCESSFUL TRADING SYSTEM

We are about to launch into the Autopilot Trading method. Before we take off, here's the high-level view. When you're flying at 30,000 feet, it's easy to see the components or sections that make up a city. Neighborhoods, roads, parks, industrial zones, transportation, and infrastructure all look different from the air. To someone who has studied multiple trading systems, there are also distinct pieces that successful systems have in common.

Systems that lack one or more of these components tend to be failures, like a city that failed to develop enough fresh water or electricity for its citizens.

Most beginning investors don't realize that <u>a plan is necessary from the beginning</u>. It's easy to open a brokerage account and throw your hard-earned money at speculative trading. Some will stumble upon a coach teaching a specific strategy. Maybe that's you...

I've seen too many investors and traders blindly follow a strategy with no system for managing the strategy. Typically, this leads to failure and significant loss of capital!

Choosing a trading system can be like choosing a city to live in. You wouldn't move without doing a little research to make sure you have everything you need in Retirementville, USA. Likewise, let's not move your capital without knowing it'll have all the structure it needs to thrive.

In my studies of different systems, I identified 6 Pillars that give any system the structure it needs to potentially be profitable (read: worthy of your attention).

The pillars rest on a basic foundation of market knowledge. Once standing, they're capped with steady returns to provide a stable structure for your wealth-growing efforts. Each pillar provides a boundary lane to help you make decisions and implement your trading rules consistently.

These are the 6 Pillars, or core components, of any successful trading system:

1. **What to trade**. Learn where to find quality entities in either stocks or ETFs. Trading junk leads to junk returns. Limit your active watchlist to no more than 25 top-quality candidates. In our case, "top quality" equals the right combination of fundamental strength, growth, movement, and clear chart signals.

2. **When and where to enter**. If you care about consistency, finding a simple, repeating pattern you trust can be the key to your financial future. Top traders like Mark Douglas and Mark Minervini agree that it's best to master one chart pattern. With a solid entry trigger, you can trade most markets with confidence and begin to master the process. Later, I'll show you exactly what I look for in a stock chart to set my profit traps.

3. **When and where to exit**. Getting in is only half the game. Before you ever buy a stock, you should have

a plan for when you will exit. You may think this is crazy, but the most important exit price is a non-negotiable stop loss. The stop loss serves as the insurance policy protecting capital from catastrophic loss. On the other side, a defined plan for taking profits drives the engine of growth and compounding. I'll address both sides in later chapters, along with my proprietary method to automate the process.

4. **What trading strategy to use**. Strategy can be as simple as buying a stock, or it can include more complex ideas like shorting stock, trading directional options, or selling option premium. In our case, we are looking at buying and selling stocks and specific ETFs. If you can master the simple, it will give you a stable platform if you choose to launch into options or other strategies with more variables.

5. **Expectations**. This is the management, tracking, and business side of trading. It actually begins by establishing a baseline expectation through backward testing and research, followed by testing in the live market. Doing the research to calculate a system's anticipated return per dollar invested and its Win:Loss ratio gives us a plumbline to measure our efforts by. The plumbline helps us make important decisions about risk management and trade planning throughout the year. In review, it provides insight into your personal trading psychology and routines. It may not sound sexy, but without this part, you are flying blind or "smoking hope-ium," as one of my early teachers said.

6. **Mentoring**. Every pilot goes through classroom studies, simulator training, and flight time with an instructor before they risk flying solo, especially

when the Navy is trusting you with a multi-million dollar jet. There's an important lesson there that applies to trading as well. Whether mentoring comes from books, videos, or one-on-one training, it matters that you get some—and that it comes from proven winners. With good mentoring added to your diligent practice, you will shorten your learning curve and get better results sooner. While you might tweak a mentor's method, you don't have to conquer the market jungles alone. If, after learning the AutoPilot Trading Method, you would like some extra help to get results faster, I have a few ways for you to engage with me and my team. Go to <u>AutoPilotTraders.com</u>, or read more about those opportunities at the end of the book.

Self-Evaluation:

Before moving on, evaluate yourself on your previous trading efforts or education.

Do you know exactly what types of stocks or securities you allow on your list? Can you briefly write out their characteristics?

Is your list small enough to manage and populated with stocks that consistently provide profit opportunities?

Are you using an objective, repeating market pattern to determine your entries? Do you know its odds of success or failure? Can it easily be confused with lower-quality signals?

Do you have a defined plan for exiting, both to protect from losses and secure profits?

Is your strategy simple and repeatable? How much effort does it require to manage open trades?

What have you come to expect from your system or education? Do you know numbers like your Win:Loss ratio and average profit or loss per trade? If not, we'll cover these things later.

Which successful traders are you learning from, or planning to learn from after you have mastered the AutoPilot Trading Method?

Up next, we will begin laying out the AutoPilot Trading Method within the six pillars framework.

CHAPTER EIGHT

PILLAR 1 - ONLY THE BEST OPPORTUNITIES BELONG ON YOUR LIST

Imagine entering a raffle and waiting with anticipation while someone pulled the winning ticket out of a basket of thousands of potential winners. If you're a bit of a strategist, you might have purchased several tickets—or several dozen—to increase your odds of winning. But it's still a shot in the dark that you'll be the big winner.

Many casual investors think of the markets in this way, and they trust that characterization from their money manager. In fact, the idea of diversification and dollar-cost-averaging relies on the same premise: that winning in the markets is largely based on chance, so the more chances you take, the higher your odds of winning. It's also lazy thinking to assume that leaving your money in for long enough means you'll just ride the overall wave of growth. And that lottery thinking comes in again, because everybody using that model hopes and prays they retire when the market is high.

But the companies that make up the markets aren't raffle tickets. Each one has its own unique characteristics that increase or decrease their potential profitability.

Companies with good potential catch the eye of investors—which impacts price.

When we talk about criterion for selecting great stocks and ETFs to trade, we need to start with the end in mind. Too many traders think that the quantity of stocks and ETFs to trade will guarantee them successful trades. This is basically unadulterated BS.

We can research the characteristics of companies that have created profitable stocks in the past and find new candidates that have similar traits now. William O'Neil proved this premise with his research and trading in the '70s and '80s, showing that high-performing stocks have had similar fundamental traits going back to the 1800's. I'd rather leave that time-consuming research to a trusted source and sort down to what I can track and what is close to being ready to trade based on technical signals.

The goal of any sorting process is to arrive at a manageable number of stocks and/or ETFs, but only those with the highest potential of profitability. Quality is always better than quantity.

I try to keep my rules to a single page. Sometimes, that means using shorthand, so for Pillar 1, my rule sheet reads "Fundamentally sound, IBD Quality Growth Stocks & Select ETFs".

Let's break that down to the core pieces so you can see what makes a good candidate for trading.

What are the most important questions to ask to get to the cream of the crop?

Two of the most important questions I asked when evaluating the stocks from each week's search are:

    1. Is the stock in the top 5 of its industry sector?

2. Does Accumulation and Distribution get a grade
    of C or better? This shows that the stock is being
    bought by institutions.

Each of these questions filters for growth stocks. Both are
answered directly in the Stock Checkup feature of Investor's
Business Daily's website at Investors.com.

You'll also find out if the stock has a relatively healthy
balance sheet and growth potential with the Stock Checkup
tool. We use a tightened-up version of William O'Neil's
guidance and *target stocks with a composite score over 95,
or Earnings Per Share EPS over 90*. We don't want to put
our money into unhealthy companies that might collapse.

A quick check lets me know immediately if a top growth
stock is fundamentally sound and worth further tracking.
This is a huge time saver! If a stock fails to meet the prelim-
inary check it is discarded from the list. At a later time, this
may change with market conditions, but taking the stock off
my list frees up time to focus on stronger candidates right
now.

My reason for wanting a high Accumulation/Distribution
rating is simply that it shows what the big money is doing.
Institutions move prices, and if we can follow in their wake,
we can profit handsomely while being nimbler.

Here are the pieces that tell me if a fundamentally strong
stock is a candidate for trading with the AutoPilot Method.

*   Share price over $10.
*   Trading volume of at least 500K shares per day for
    liquidity.
*   Charts with observable price patterns.

You might also consider the availability and liquidity of
options on an entity if you choose to go that route. For now,

these few core criteria tell me if a stock is a potential candidate for my list.

ETFs can be a little simpler. On those, I look for:
1. Liquidity - 500K shares per day or more.
2. Multiple opportunities to potentially compound trades to 100% per year. I gauge this by looking at the chart and doing some quick measurements. (This is only measuring potential; it shows me there's plenty of swing to meet my actual goals.)

Very few ETFs meet that second test, which keeps my list small. You can download a list of my favorites at AutoPilot-Traders.com/Print-Resources. This page will give you free access to a library of tools and tutorials worth over $500 with the coupon code PRINT100. If I could only trade on ETF, in my opinion, the best one to trade regularly is a leveraged version of the Nasdaq 100, ticker: TQQQ.

I'll repeat: **quality is always better than quantity**. It doesn't matter how many great stocks are on your list if you can't manage them.

So, what's a manageable number?

Focus is the key here. If you focus on only the best candidates, you'll trade better. If you let inferior opportunities clutter up your attention, your results will suffer.

Typically, successful traders refine their list to somewhere between 5 and perhaps 10 stocks or ETFs at any one time. If you have extra time, you MIGHT be able to track 25 targets. But I strongly recommend against going higher. I've been there and it's not what you want.

So how does one go from 500 or 600 stocks from multiple watch lists and arrive at between 5 and 25 stocks of primary interest?

The way I do it is to find a pool of the most fundamentally sound stocks and then find the strongest within this pool. For ETFs, I focus on either index ETFs or a few sector ETFs to provide a small pool of quality targets.

Cutting Down to the Best Candidates

What's my quick shortcut for finding a good pool of fundamentally sound growth stocks?

I outsource that basic research to Investors Business Daily (IBD) at Investors.com. They're a research outlet with a proven track record of finding stocks that beat the market. IBD provides 14 premium watchlists each week that form the foundation of my weekly searches. The flagship list is the IBD 50 which is updated multiple times per week and has a decades-long track record of beating the indices.

I find that I increase the probability of finding winning trades when I fish where the big fish swim. The IBD 50 and the other 14 premium watch lists guarantee that I am fishing in the right ponds.

From there, I cull that list until I get to the best of the best. But it's easier than you might think with modern tools.

Every Friday, I do a sort on those watchlists, using the more strict metrics I mentioned above. I learned about the benefit of tightening the fundamental requirements from my friend and fellow IBD Meetup leader, Lee Tanner, from Petaluma, CA. This sort guarantees that the five or six strongest fundamental stocks are always in focus going into the new week. What I found over the years is that the IBD

50 watchlist always provides market-beating stocks. Many of these stocks go on to achieve high double-digit and even triple-digit gains during the year. And they often follow the repeatable patterns I trade.

It doesn't happen every time, but it does happen all the time. Often enough that William O'Neil built an empire on these types of stocks.

The IBD stock sort I do every weekend allows me to go through all 14 premium IBD watchlists in an hour. In that time, I whittle those hundreds of stocks down to what I call the "Power Rank Elite" Watchlist.

My simple sort to get down to the top 15-25 candidates for the week is to compare all of the lists from IBD and narrow my group to only those that show up on at least four of those lists. I use an Excel spreadsheet to simplify the process.

First, I paste all 14 lists into my spreadsheet, and then perform a simple sort in Excel to find the duplicates among the lists. If a stock shows up on at least four lists, I add it to my "Power Rank Elite" Watchlist.

From there, I go to the Stock Checkup tool at IBD and quickly check each of those 15-25 stocks against the two questions I said were most important.

1. Is the stock in the top 5 of its industry sector?
2. Does Accumulation and Distribution get a grade of C or better?

They usually pass, but if any sneak through the initial sort, I cull them here. The check on Composite Score and EPS is an easy third-level checkup while I'm there, but I'm not quite as strict with those metrics.

These sorts are based on specific criteria for growth stocks highlighted in William O'Neil's book, *How to Make Money in Stocks*, like some of the ones mentioned above. However, as I said, my friend Lee tightened up the criteria even more based on his research and then taught me his method. I've added my own twists for my way of trading.

The process above gets me down to my starting list for the week, and then I move on to my technical analysis. We'll cover that in the next chapter. For now, I'll just say that technical analysis on these 15-25 stocks usually highlights a mere handful that are showing potential for a trade in the next week.

The results of this process provide the 4 or 5 fundamentally strongest stocks appearing on the IBD 50 each week.

In honor of Lee, I guess I can call this the Lee Tanner sort. I have noticed one of the most important aspects of this process is that often, the same fundamentally strongest stocks appear over multiple weeks, giving me even more confidence in these opportunities.

The main takeaway from this exercise is that the stocks that earn their way to the fundamentally strongest list tend to outperform the market.

I can trust I'm considering only the best trading candidates with the most opportunity.

As part of your purchase of this book, I've included a few video tutorials to help demonstrate and flesh out some of the technical concepts. If you need a little more clarity on the process described above, including a walkthrough of my sort, you can get a full video tutorial at AutoPilotTraders.com/Print-Resources. Again, you have free access to this library of tools and tutorials with the coupon code PRINT100.

However, if you're too busy to go through this process, that's exactly the situation that led me to create my AutoPilot Trading Service. Members of the service get the list of the 5 stocks I'm looking at trading each week, along with exactly where I'm placing orders, like I'll explain in the next chapter. There's a lot more included with the service, but it's one way I try to help people like you get results faster. If you're curious, you can learn more about the service at AutoPilotTraders.com.

Now that we have a list of the best stocks, Pillar 1 is securely planted. We can move on to Pillar 2: When and where to buy.

But we don't just snatch them up as soon as we see them.

Waiting for proper entry triggers on these market leaders is half the battle if we want to actually make money.

In the next few chapters, we'll explain the simple three-step setup that reveals the VAZs where we want to set our traps.

Review:

- The best stock opportunities share these traits:
- In the top 5 of its industry sector.
    - Accumulation and Distribution rating of at least C, showing it's being bought by institutions.
    - IBD composite score over 95+ and EPS over 85.
    - Over $10 per share.
    - Trade over 500k shares per day.
    - Show the price patterns I want to trade.

- ETFs need:
    - Liquidity (>500k shares/day).

- o Price patterns with large enough moves to potentially compound at 100% per year.

    - Focus on the best candidates!
        - o Limit your watch list to 5-10 candidates at any given time.
    - Save time by outsourcing some of the research.
        - o Find pools of stocks with acceptable fundamentals
        - o Cherry-pick the best with sorts and tools that make it easy to check their fundamental quality.

Practice:

Check your current list. Does it meet the criteria above?

If you're not currently fishing where the big fish swim, where will you look for a pool of these quality stocks?

Consider how much time it takes you to evaluate one stock for trading. Ask yourself how much time you want to devote to research each week or month. With that time constraint, how many stocks can you realistically watch?

CHAPTER NINE

PILLAR 2 - THE "3-STEP" PRECISION ENTRY POINTS ROUTINE

To buy and hold investors, chart reading sounds like a mystical effort to predict the future. It's like reading tea leaves or omens.

In reality, charts are just visual representations that show the value decisions of buyers and sellers. But somewhere, somebody figured out that those charts reveal repeating patterns of behavior. Since human nature never changes, people end up being predictable—especially in groups.

That predictability means those repeating patterns reveal opportunities in the market. Over a large enough sample size, each pattern develops a statistical probability of the price going higher or lower after it shows up. That means you can "predict" the likelihood of a price direction using math.

Or, as I've said before: It doesn't happen every time, but it does happen all the time.

I've spent years studying thick books on all types of chart patterns and technical indicators. And when you have so many possible signals to trade on, it really does feel like a mystical exercise in reading omens. The multiplicity of trading indicators often provides conflicting information.

These days, I prefer to take my own advice on focus. So, I narrowed my attention onto the few elements that I can see easily on charts (it gets harder with age) and have proven from my research to have a high likelihood of achieving the results I want in profits for time I spend trading.

Remember a few chapters back when we talked about **Value Action Zones**? This chapter will cover what that means on the entry side of trading. Since it's technical, it will be one of the longer chapters. But ultimately, I've boiled my entries down to a 3-step setup routine that I like to call my Precision Entry Point Routine (PEP Routine). It takes advantage of visual markers on the chart that allow you to set precise targets for your entries and your exits—at the same time. Once you see those markers, you can't argue whether a trade opportunity fits the system.

(You still might have to argue with yourself about whether you're going to take it, but that deals with your psychology, a topic for later.)

You may have heard others, like Mark Douglas, call this a "Mechanical Setup", or a setup based on the visual chart of market behavior. Everybody has their name for it because the idea has been around for a long time. The most important concept is that you want to focus on ONE market trigger to really hone your skills and start getting results.

CHART INTERPRETATION: *When you're reading charts, the combination of conditions will offer one of three interpretations:*

1) Time to wait – either the setup or trigger has not occurred,

2) Ready to trade – the setup is visible and I've placed orders in my Value Action Zone, or

3) Time to exit – when I'm in a trade, my rules tell me where to place exit orders.

Our 3-Step PEP Routine uses as few indicators as possible to avoid distractions. It focuses on Price Action and Momentum, which helps us decide on the Trigger that executes our entry.

Captured in a nutshell, I'm looking for bullish reversal patterns at a price level of support, coupled with my momentum indicator being oversold or at its own bullish level of support. (Bullish levels of support on indicators often appear after the longer-term uptrend has commenced. Both price and momentum will be pulling back as shorter-term traders are taking some profits off the table. I'll show examples later.)

Traders will dramatically increase the probability of a profitable trade if they focus on the following three parameters.

1. Price
2. Momentum
3. Triggers

To draw it in the most generic form, it would look something like this:

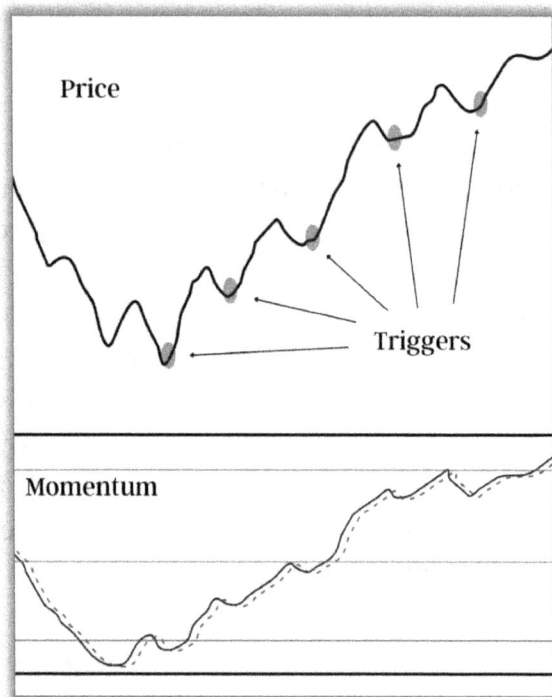

We'll cover the examples and specifics, but it boils down to those 3 things. The setup can occur at multiple places along a trend, but it will always include clues on the price, momentum, and then a specific trigger point.

The PEP Routine is the most important piece of the puzzle for Pillar 2: When and Where to Enter.

Price Action:

I'm looking for setup clues on daily and weekly charts.

Trend: Identify the short and long-term trends—either up, down, or sideways. Favor the long-term trend until there is clear evidence of a trend reversal.

Trade up in an uptrend. If you like trading to the downside, do that in downtrends, or keep your powder dry.

The trend doesn't specifically create the setup but tells us where our sentiment should be.

Location: Where is the price in relation to key moving averages? Is price action taking place above or below the 50-day moving average? (Simple (SMA) and Exponential (EMA) are both acceptable).

When price is above the 50-day average, you should have more confidence in bullish signals and their probability of success.

If it's below the 50-day average, it's likely been in a recent decline. Exercise appropriate caution with signals. We'll discuss in later chapters what that caution looks like.

Is there a nearby area of support or resistance? When price repeatedly stops or reverses at a particular area on the chart, we call that area "support" (a floor) or "resistance" (a ceiling). It shows where buyers or sellers are willing to step in, and it is a powerful tool.

I often say, "Look to left." Current levels of Support and Resistance are usually due to levels of Support and Resistance from the past. Thus, looking to the left from current price action can show potential levels where price action may stop or reverse from the current trend. Additionally, if a past level of Support or Resistance has been identified, one can be more observant of candlestick reversal signals at and around these past levels. See the chart below.

CLUES FROM MULTIPLE TIMEFRAMES: *Also be aware of Support and Resistance levels identified on various timeframe charts. Some levels on a Weekly Chart may not be obvious on a Daily Chart and vice versa. This is a truism for every chart timeframe.*

Support and resistance can be horizontal (at a specific area of price), diagonal (following an imaginary line during a trend), or dynamic (something like a moving average).

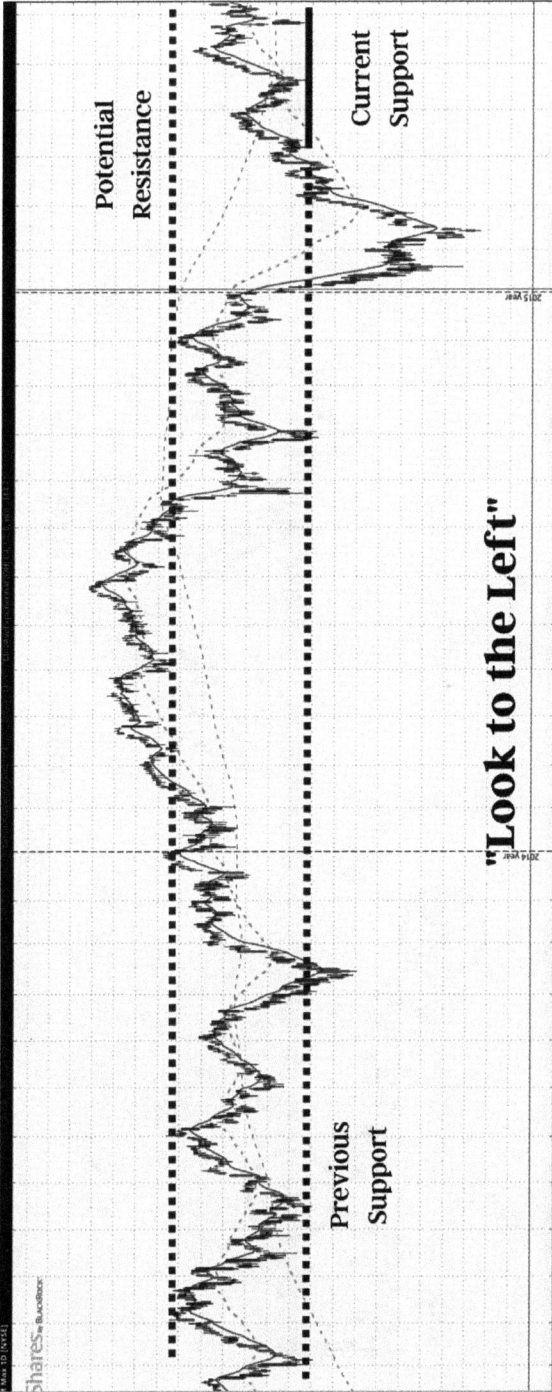

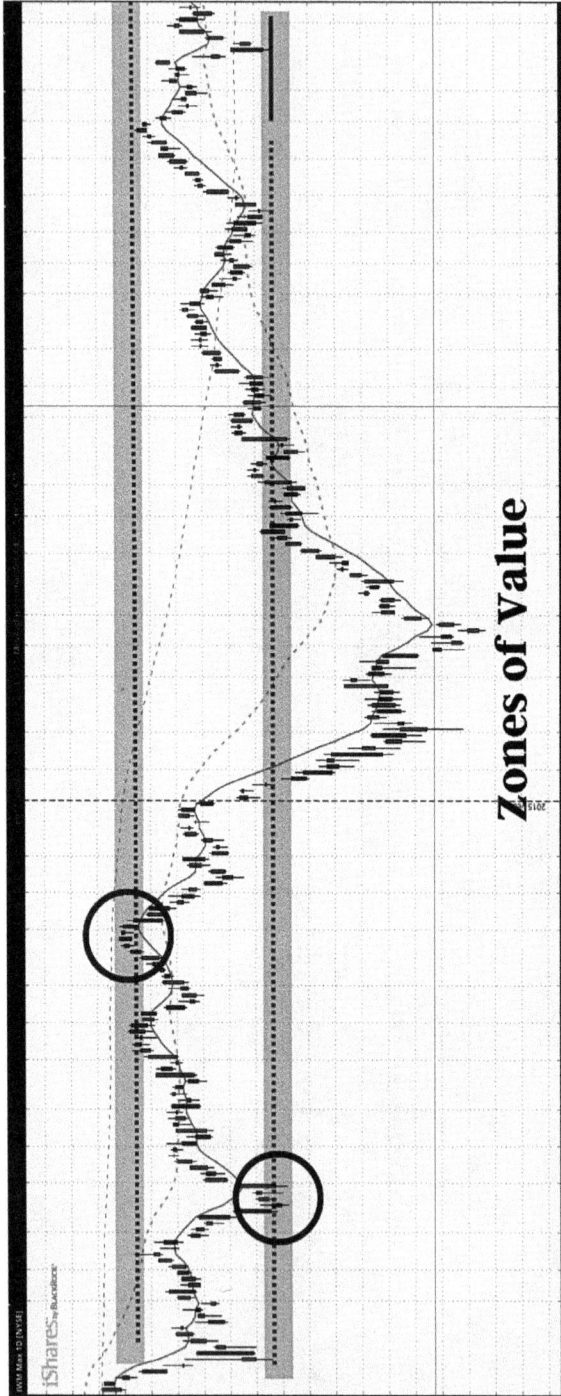

Zones of Value: Another way to think about support and resistance is what one of the fathers of technical analysis, Richard Wyckoff, called Value Action Zones. In his model, they represented areas of supply and demand. At support, prices are low, and buyers show up, increasing demand and forcing prices higher. At resistance, prices are high, and sellers want to cash out, increasing the supply and often leading to prices softening.

The important thing is that these are "zones," NOT specific levels. Support and resistance are often price ranges instead of precise amounts. Keep this concept in mind as you consider where to place your trade orders for entry and exits. Notice how the exact price line works most of the time but that prices occasionally hover around it, creating an **area of support or resistance**.

Refer to the example charts above, but we'll cover more detail and nuance in the bonus videos that came with the book at AutoPilotTraders.com/Print-Resources. Remember the coupon code: PRINT100.

Reversal Candles: Is there a reversal candlestick on a weekly or daily chart that lands at or near past support after a downtrend (correction) or pullback (slight drop in an uptrend)?

You can set your chart to different representations for price on a daily or weekly basis. We prefer candlesticks. They look like a candle, usually with a "wick" sticking out of the top and bottom. They instantly show you the open, close, high, and low prices for that day or week. On bullish candles, the open is the bottom of the body, and the close is the top, meaning prices went up that day from where they started. Bearish candles reverse this.

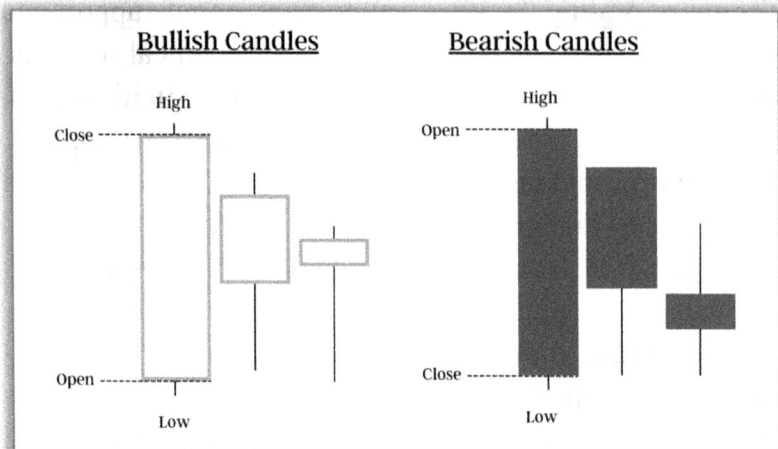

Most charting software lets you add color to your candles, like green for positive days, red for negative days. When you see monochrome charts, up days usually show the outline only, while down days are filled in. In the real chart examples in this book, you will see lighter shaded candles as up days and darker shaded candles as down days.

The candlesticks in the figure above are just examples of what they can look like. (Candlesticks can also be set for intraday timeframes, but that's an advanced technique. For our style of trading, anything less than 30-minute candles adds confusion and noise. Not recommended.)

More importantly, a handful of candlestick shapes reveal the sentiment between buyers and sellers if you know how to read them. They can create their own patterns with statistical probabilities of prices going higher or lower—revealing a piece of evidence for a Value Action Zone, and sometimes offering extremely precise targeting.

There are dozens of recognized candlestick patterns.

I believe only 7 are worth your time.
- 6 primary patterns
- 1 indecision pattern

Below is a chart of the 7 I recommend learning. You can find more detail about these candlestick signals in the appendix, or with a video tutorial at <u>AutoPilotTraders.com/Print-Resources</u>. (PRINT100).

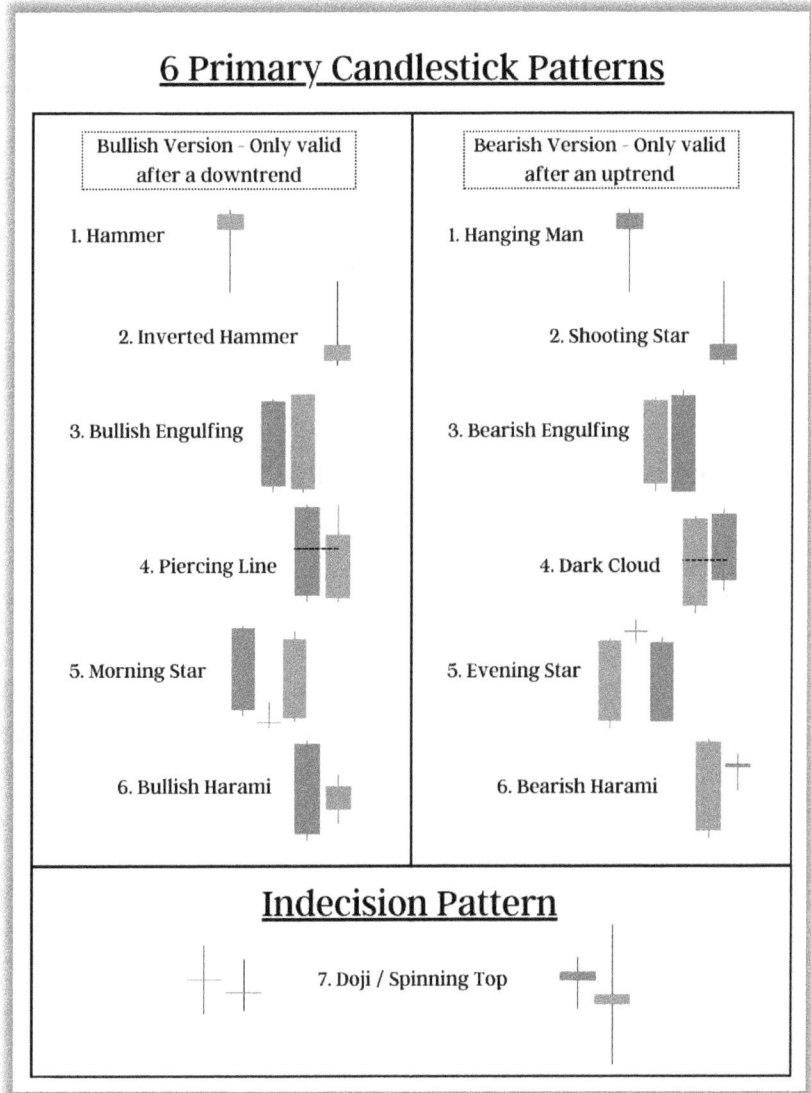

6 Primary Candlestick Patterns

Bullish Version - Only valid after a downtrend	Bearish Version - Only valid after an uptrend
1. Hammer	1. Hanging Man
2. Inverted Hammer	2. Shooting Star
3. Bullish Engulfing	3. Bearish Engulfing
4. Piercing Line	4. Dark Cloud
5. Morning Star	5. Evening Star
6. Bullish Harami	6. Bearish Harami

Indecision Pattern

7. Doji / Spinning Top

Confirmation: A question that often comes up is whether a candlestick reversal signal needs confirmation. As with so many things in trading the answer is, "It depends." Mostly on your own tolerances.

Candlestick trigger confirmations are often covered by the next period's price action. Waiting for confirmation can be a sound approach because supporting momentum and moving average crosses have also been triggered. Every so often, multiple candlesticks will appear to be repeated reversal signals, but then they turn into a holding pattern where bulls and bears fight for control. The longer a move drifts sideways without confirming that original candlestick, the more caution you should exercise.

If the Momentum (TSI) indicator is at oversold extremes, then taking a trade on the initial reversal signal can be prudent because prices may gap away after the signal. Just be sure to manage your risk appropriately on these early triggers. That is something we'll cover in a later chapter.

Momentum Shifts:

Stocks that go nowhere don't make you money. Momentum is where the money is made. I use a simple, 2-line indicator called the True Strength Index (TSI) to show when momentum is shifting and opportunities are about to show up.

Two of my Texas trading buddies first introduced me to the TSI. I was intrigued by how well it moved similarly to both Stochastic and RSI oscillators. The Engineer in me saw that the factory settings on the TSI were good but could be improved to provide more timely momentum shift clues. I adjusted TSI to (8,8,3 Exponential, 42) for ThinkorSwim charts.

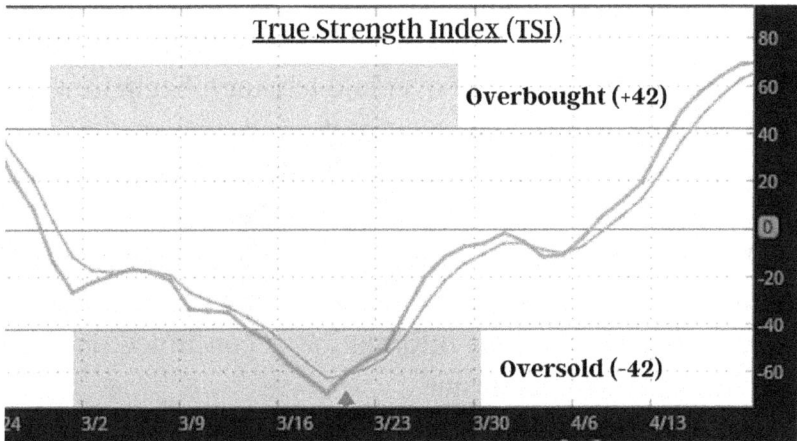

TSI has a midline at 0, and with my chart setup, it's considered oversold at -42 and overbought at +42. When the stock has pushed itself to one of those extremes, a tradeable reversal becomes much more likely. However, when the stock is on a prolonged trend, TSI also has its own common levels of support or resistance where I can look for momentum shift clues. Those levels vary from chart to chart, but almost all charts will use the 0 line as one area of support or resistance.

THE TRUE STRENGTH INDEX (TSI) *is an excellent Momentum Indicator. Traders should look for 3 Major Setup Signals from TSI and then look for supporting or converging clues such as reversal candlesticks patterns, support/resistance levels and price action trends.*

For a more in-depth tutorial on TSI, go to AutoPilotTrad-ers.com/Print-Resources. Get it for free with the code PRINT100.

The three TSI conditions that I consider clues for a setup:

1. Oversold: Bottoming at extremes & reversing – When both TSI lines are below the -42 line, the entity is considered Oversold. When you're in oversold territory, begin to watch for a reversal candle near or at past price support. Once the reversal candle is complete, TSI should start rolling up and may even cross to the upside the same day.

A valid setup appears when TSI begins reversing toward the upside. This tells me the market's in a position to consider bullish trades. This information is confirmed once the two lines cross to the upside.

For the strongest setups, weekly and daily Momentum should be in sync. While daily Momentum will be more sensitive, falling momentum on a weekly chart often retards any price reversal on the daily. Trade with caution. However, when weekly or monthly Momentum is extremely oversold, a reversal can potentially lead to a significant and prolonged upside move.

2. Positive Divergence: A lower low on price with a higher low on TSI – This can be one of the strongest and highest probability setups, especially if the higher low is still below -42. (The opposite would be negative divergence and is a warning sign of a potential bearish reversal.)

Positive divergence shows that price action is at or below past levels of support, but Momentum has already shifted into a bullish posture. This is often followed by an explosive trend reversal. A positively divergent chart is prone to a "gap-and-go" action that sees rapid short-term gains.

3. Trend-Continuation Support Bounce: Once a new trend has been established, TSI will pull back with price action. Prices will often pull back towards the 8, 20, or 50-day Moving Averages (MAs) as short-term traders take profits. A common pattern is for the price to pull back approximately 3-4 times during a significant trend. During these price action pullbacks TSI will also return to support levels and then reverse when price action bounces off of dynamic support. Most often, TSI will reverse near either the +20, 0, or -20 ranges. Occasionally, it uses the oversold and overbought lines for support as well. If price action is trending, TSI location and slope can provide a trader with clues of an upcoming bounce and longer-term trend continuation.

Notice in the example that price is bouncing off moving averages or support in "flag" patterns that we will talk about again.

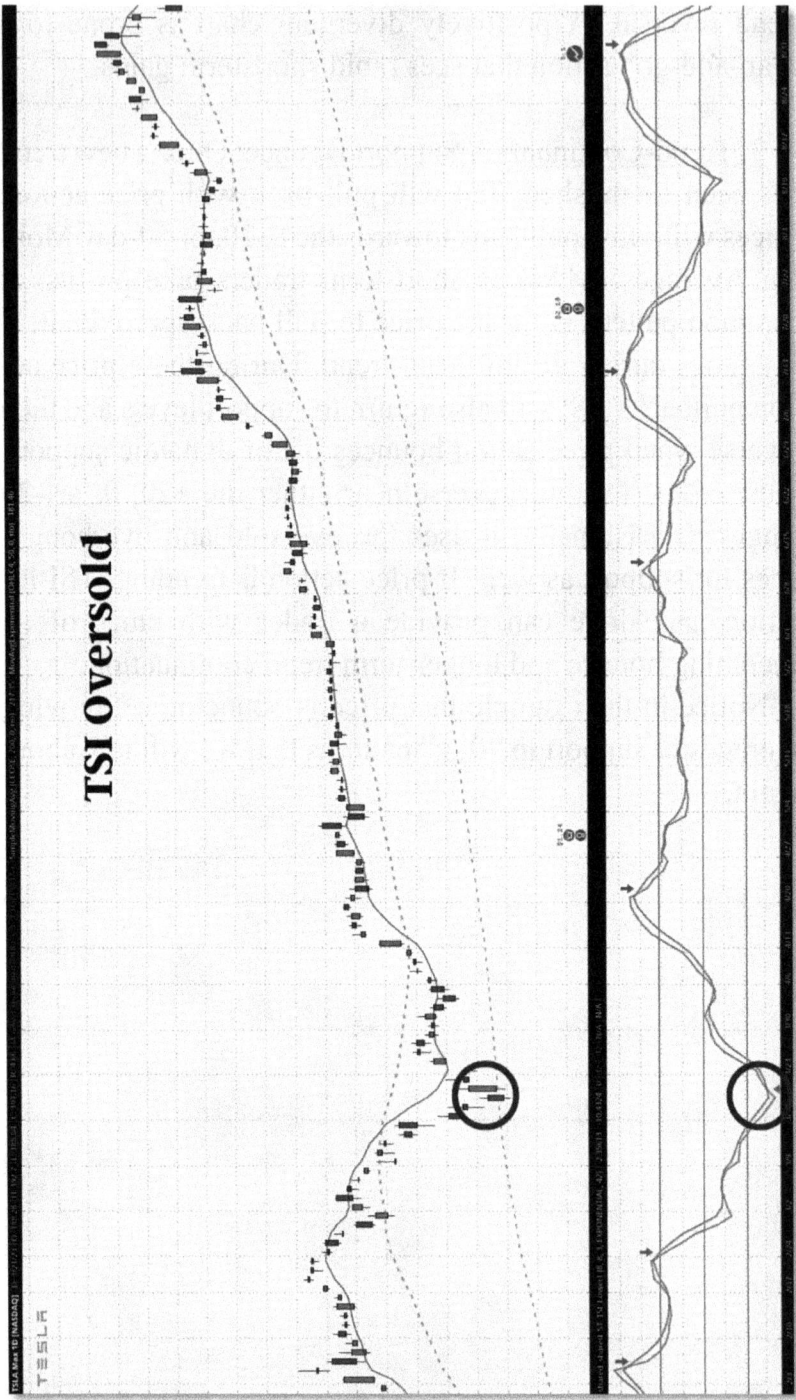

TSI Oversold

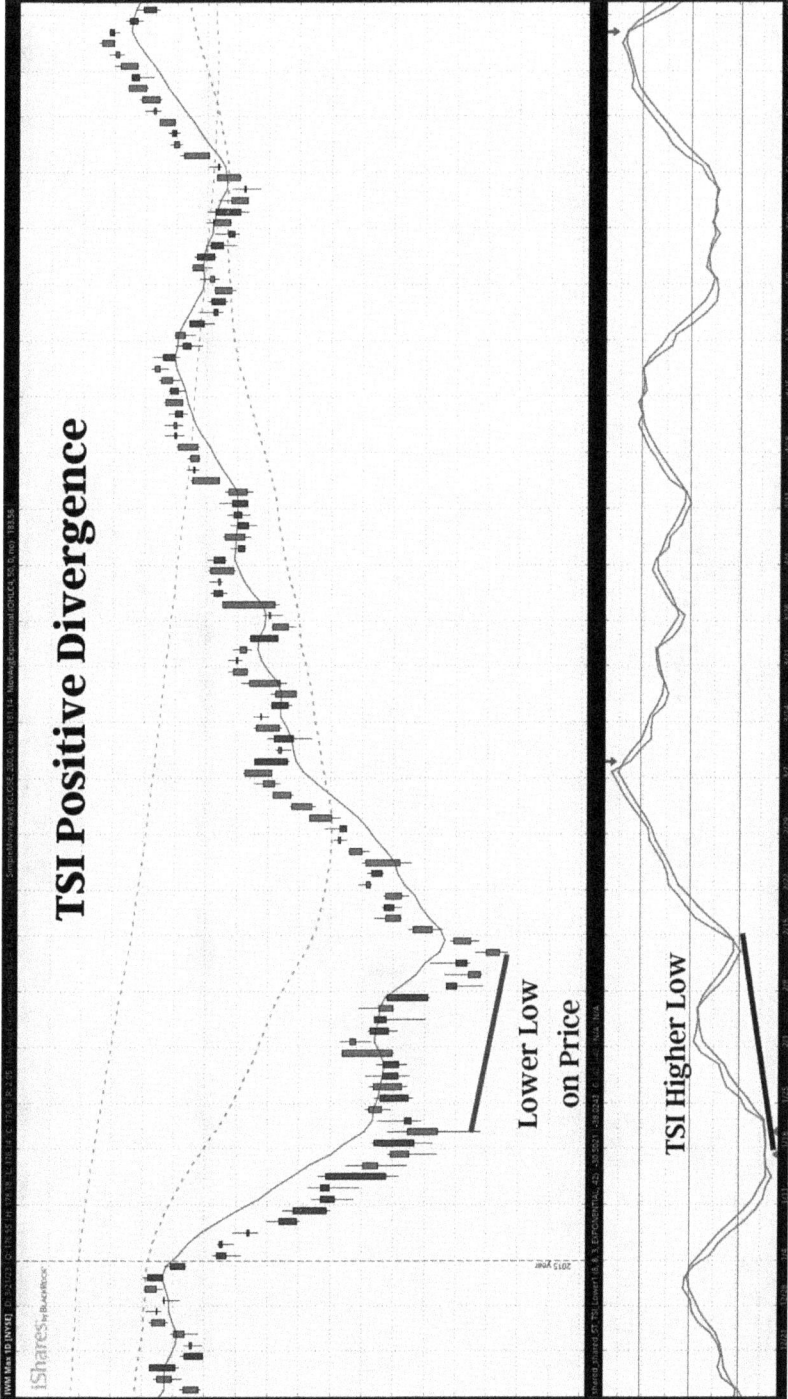

TSI Positive Divergence

Lower Low on Price

TSI Higher Low

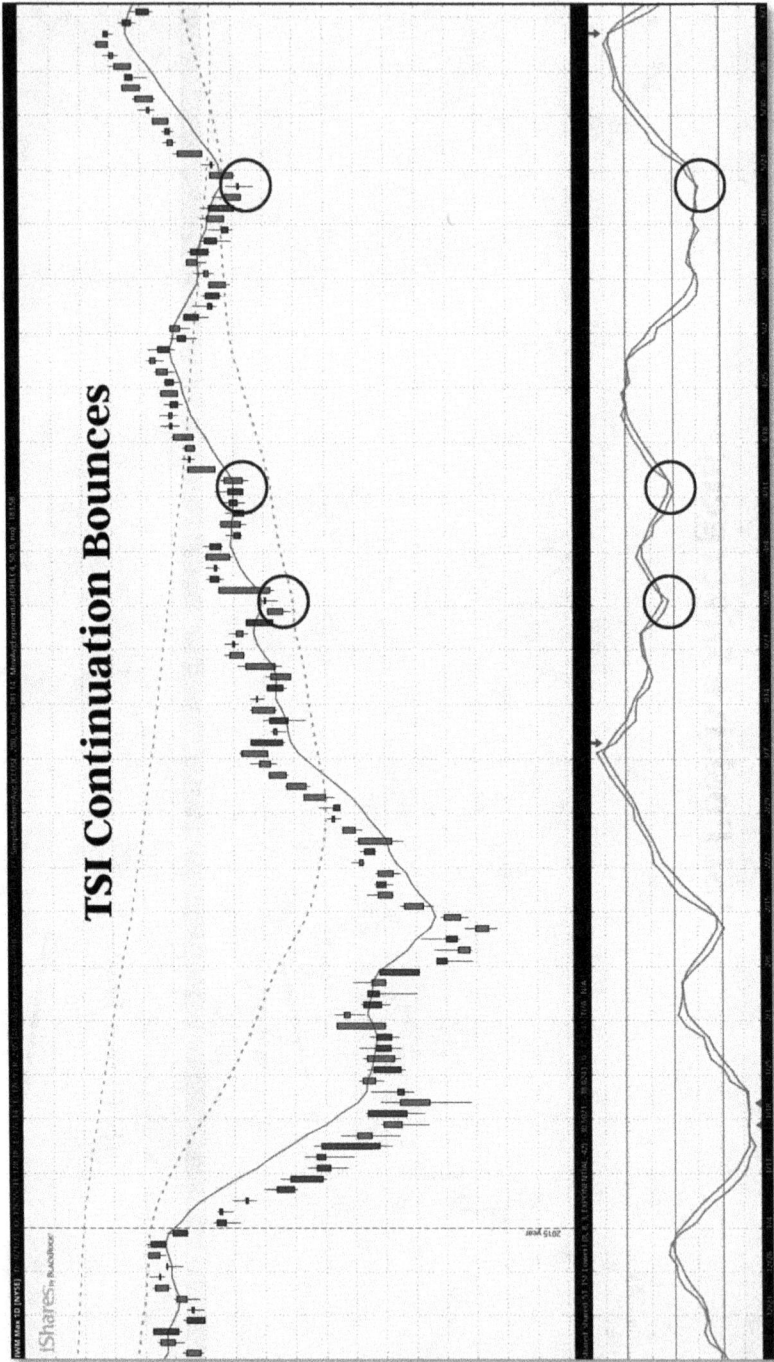

TSI Continuation Bounces

To learn more about the nuances of the TSI and my personal settings, find the video at AutoPilotTraders.com/Print-Resources. Once again, use the coupon code PRINT100 for free access. You'll also find another option for oscillators that give a couple more clues on setups.

The chart is telling me I'm ready to trade when I see:
1. Price near a support zone
2. Confirmed reversal candlesticks
3. Momentum (TSI) in one of the above conditions

The next step is deciding on my trigger so I can place my trade traps.

Triggers:

There are a few potential options for pinpointing your entry price when you see a setup coming together. Remember, there is no such thing as a perfect setup or entry! Partly because price bounces around in Zones (VAZs) and partly because each trader has different goals and a different interpretation of the data. The edge comes from the high-probability nature of the PEP Routine setup and accompanying triggers. If you can identify the setup consistently and execute on the triggers, the odds will be in your favor statistically over the long-term.

Here are my specific triggers for the AutoPilot Trading method.

Trigger 1: Early - Before momentum has turned up, you may enter after seeing a reversal candlestick (a Bullish Engulfing in the chart of Trigger 1). Enter as close to support as possible (10-20 cents) with proper confirmation of that candle pattern. This is a bet that the candle reversal will bend momentum with it. (This trigger may put you closer to the ultimate bottom, increasing your potential wins, but with the chance of more trades stopping out in an area of volatility. It's about your tolerance.)

Trigger 2: Momentum Turn- Near support after the momentum has turned up from oversold or is crossing up from a short-term price action pullback. Again, within 10-20 cents of support. Look for hidden levels of support on different timeframe charts. In the Trigger 2 example chart, TSI is positively divergent, which means that it's putting in a higher low while the price has not yet made a higher low. At the right edge, we see two candles with a hammer-type shape.

Trigger 3: Close Above 8-Day - After momentum has turned up, when the price closes above the 8-day exponential moving average (EMA). Closing above the 8-day EMA after the shift in momentum provides both a trigger and strong confirmation that an uptrend is continuing or starting. Enter near the close of the day, or as close as possible to the 8-day, since a retest will often occur the following day. In the example for Trigger 3, there are no specific candle signals at support, so the close above the 8-day is what gives us the confidence to trade.

The first three triggers are observed most frequently after significant pullbacks or prolonged downtrends. If you're coming to a chart in an uptrend, then use trigger 4. From a

TSI perspective, crossing the red "0" line in the middle confirms a change in trend. If the chart is showing a rising TSI that crosses above 0, look for trigger 4.

$|_{+}\mathord{\mathring{\mathsf{q}}}\mathsf{|}\mathord{\mathsf{\mathring{q}}}$

Trigger 4: Flags in Existing Uptrend - During a new or existing uptrend, look to trade bounces off the 8, 20, or 50-period EMA as support. You will often see short-term momentum and sometimes candlesticks confirming these areas to trade. We often refer to these short pullbacks as "flags". In the Trigger 4 Chart below, the price repeatedly drops down toward the 50-day MA with relative control. These aren't massive crashes. Each time it creates one of these flags, it rebounds to a new, higher high before repeating the pattern. When you see this pattern, you're still looking for support, candlesticks, and a momentum shift. We enter as close to support as possible and follow the rules on position sizing and risk management in Chapter 12.

See the four chart examples on the following pages.

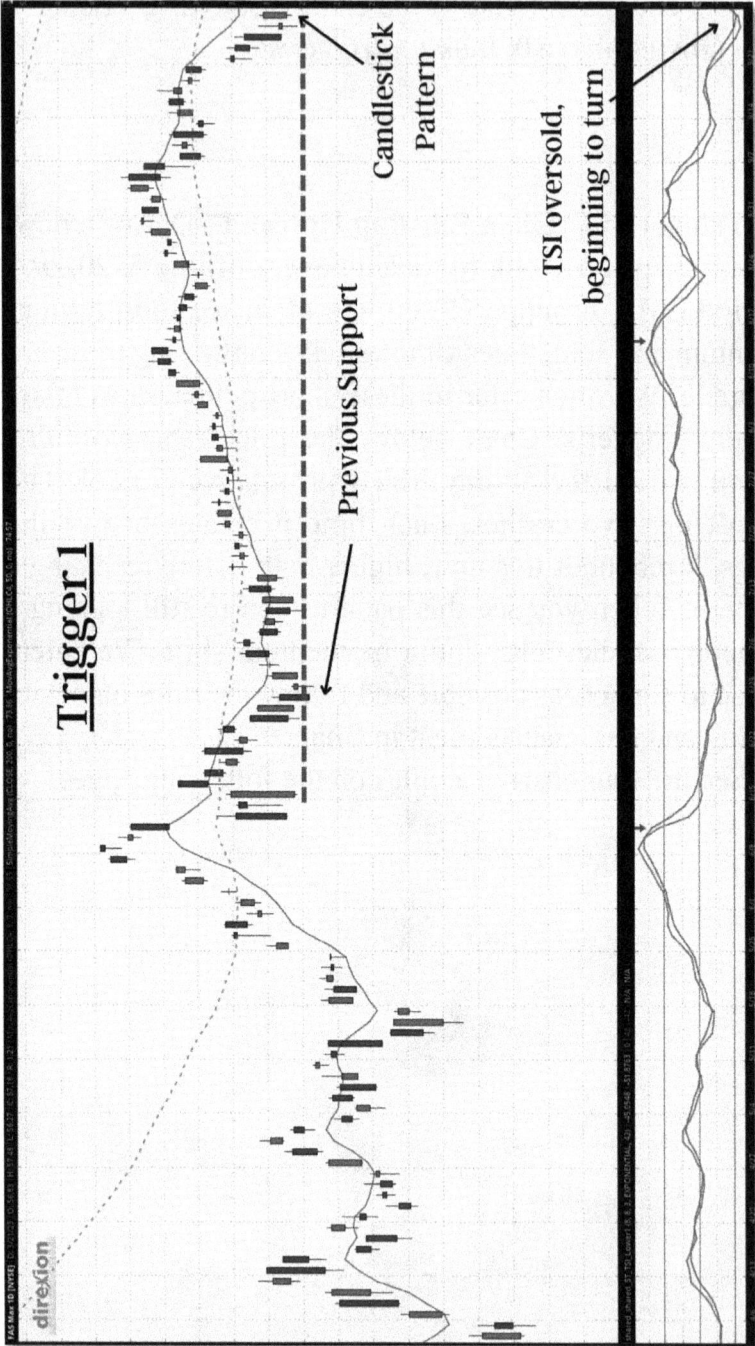

Trigger 2

Candlestick Pattern

TSI turned, now bouncing off support & divergence

Previous Support

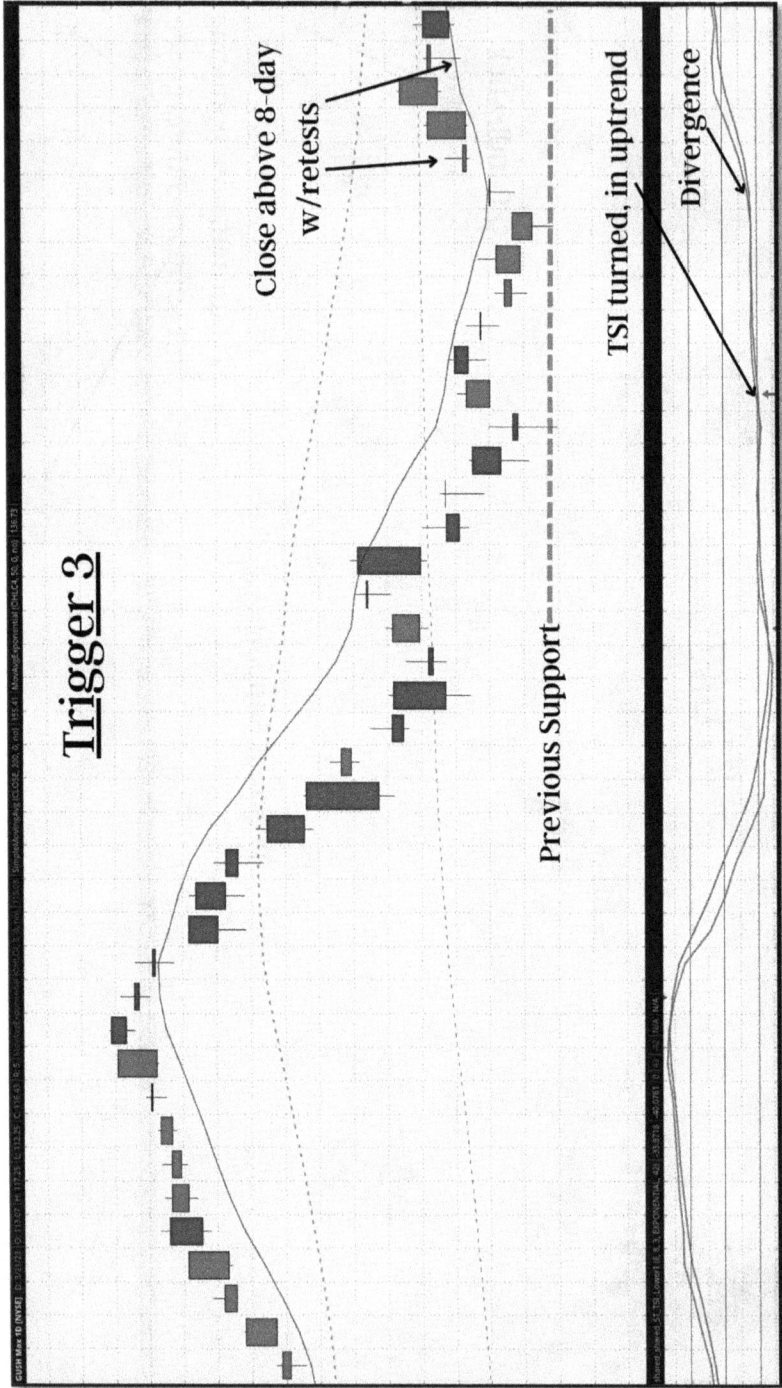

Trigger 3

Close above 8-day w/retests

Previous Support

TSI turned, in uptrend

Divergence

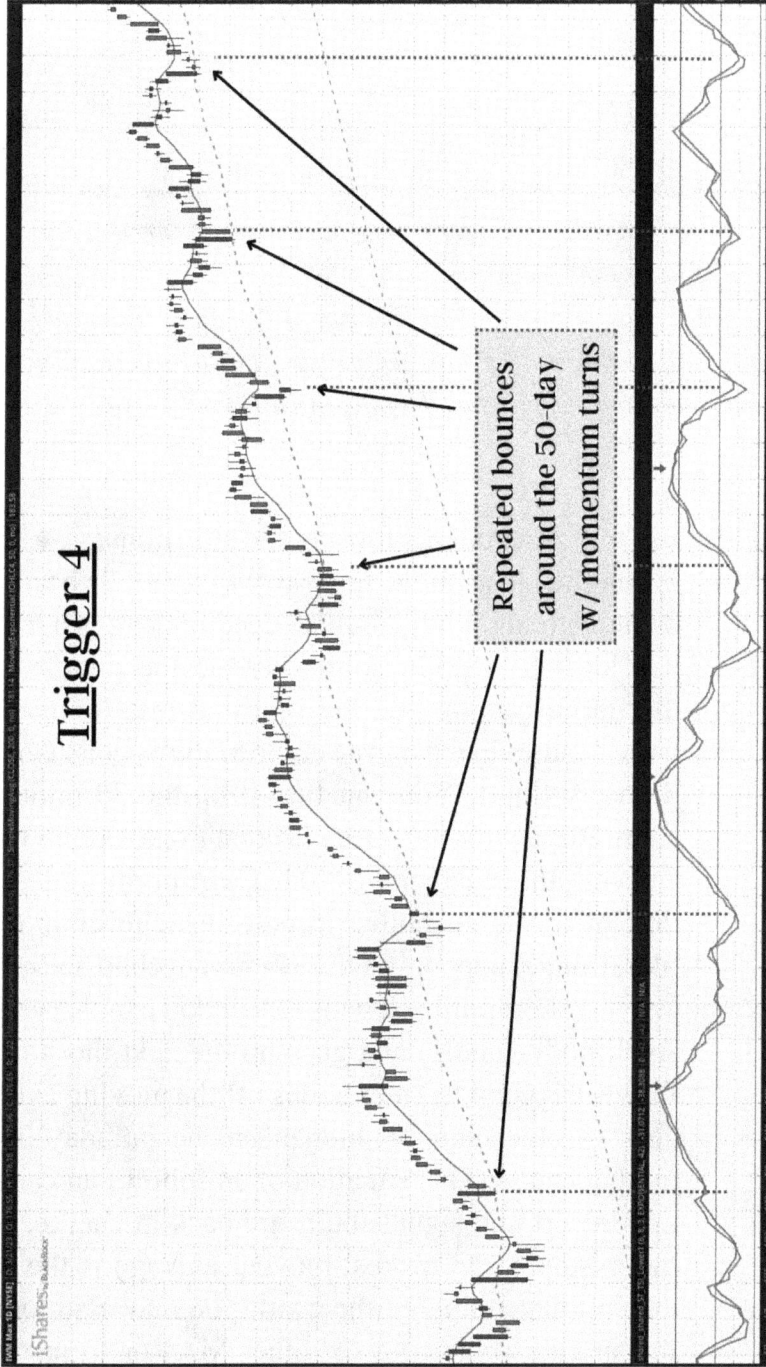

Trigger 4

Repeated bounces around the 50-day w/ momentum turns

|₊ᶲ|ᶲ

FLAGS: *You can see in the chart labeled "Flags", that these flags look like brief pullbacks toward the ongoing trend or moving averages. They can be steep or shallow in angle. They can be clearly defined with a line across the tops, or they can be a bit sloppy and harder to track. Each chart will have its own feel to the flag pattern. After the market moves into a significant bullish trend, this is the trigger you will see more often.*

I also use two adjustments for specific situations.

    A. When the close above the 8-day (Trigger 3) occurs on an extremely large bullish candle, there is a hidden level of support somewhere in the middle of that large candle. See the repeated tests of these large candles in the purple circle of the Special Condition A Chart. You can find it on the 30-minute chart. Place your order trap (a conditional order) 10-20 cents above either the 8-day EMA or the midsection of the large bullish candle, whichever looks like stronger support on the 30-minute chart setting.

    B. When a short pullback ends with a doji candle (very small body candle) and gaps up the next morning, follow trigger 4 to enter trades off the moving averages or other support hidden on the intraday 30-minute charts. This situation often follows an earnings report and signals bulls are back in charge. In the example, the nearest moving average is the 8-day but depending on the chart, you may also look for an entry bouncing off other MAs or from old swing highs that were previously resistance.

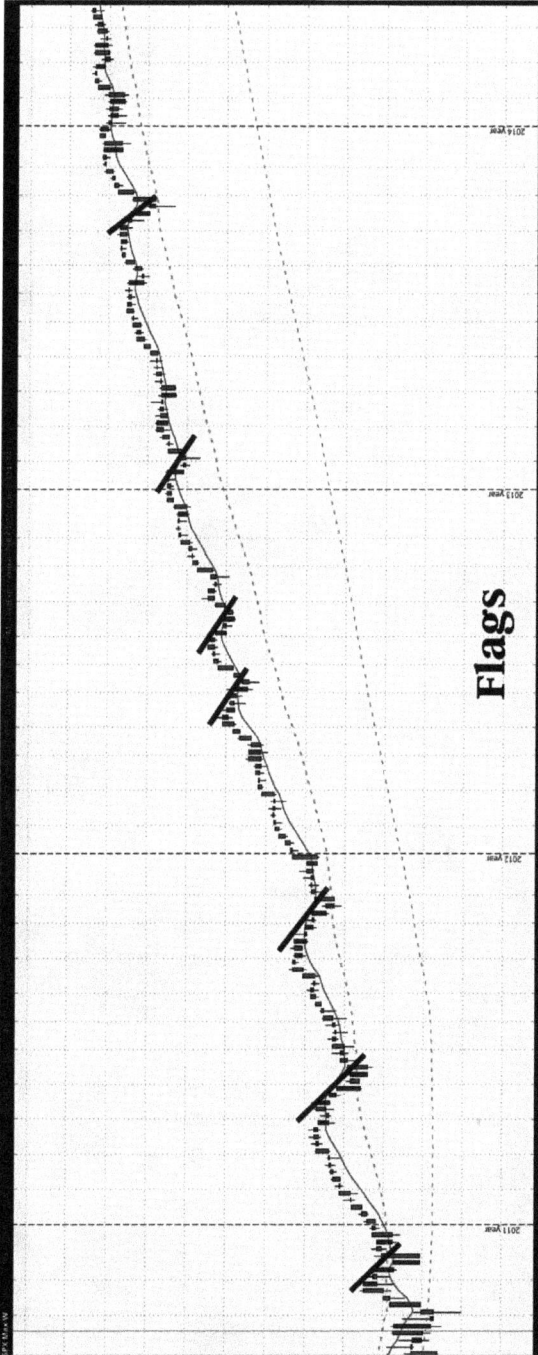

Special Condition A: Large Candles

Midsection of Large Candles repeatedly tested

Bottom of Large Candles often tested

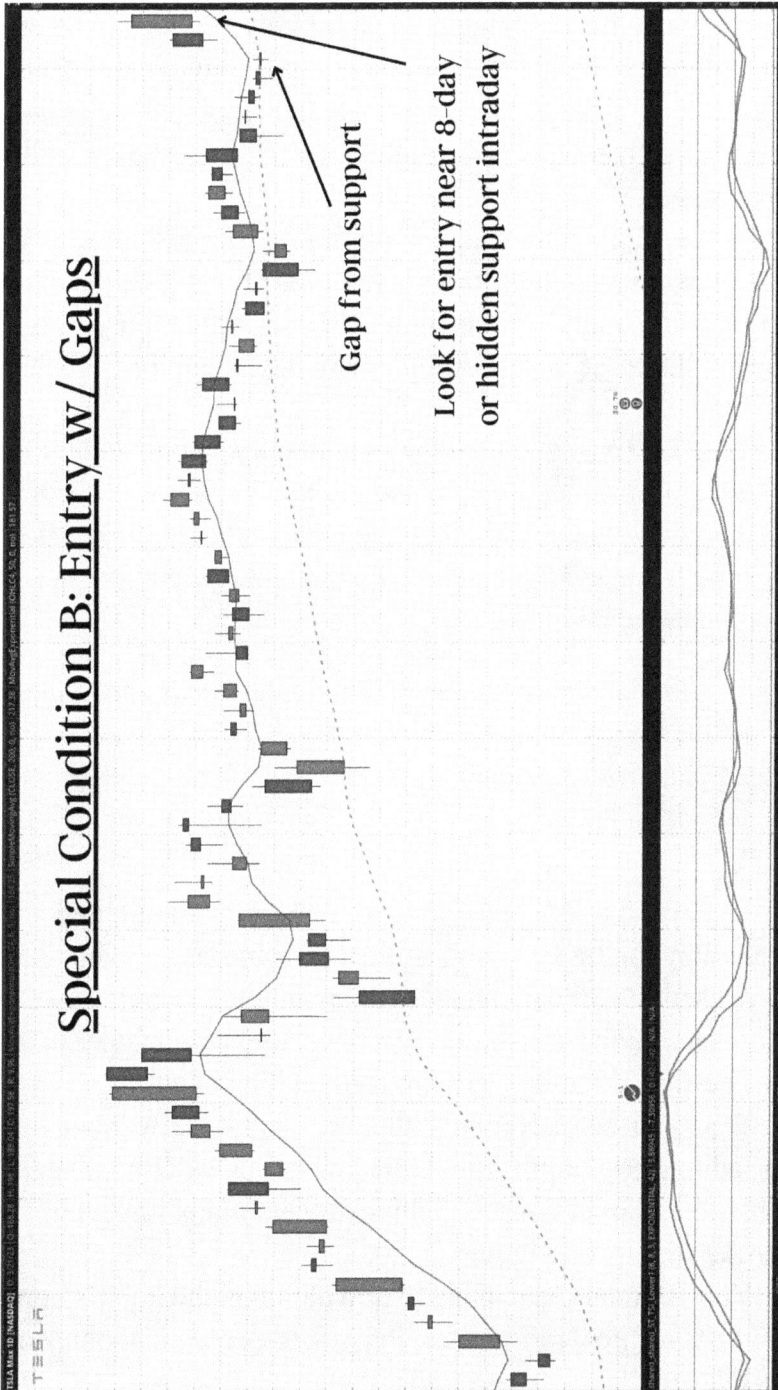

Special Condition B: Entry w/ Gaps

Gap from support

Look for entry near 8-day
or hidden support intraday

The early birds (Trigger 1) will likely see higher returns on individual trades but face more whipsaw (when trades rapidly turn against your direction and stop out). That hurts their Win:Loss ratio and requires a very steady psychology to manage.

If you decide to trade these initial signals after a big downturn, watch the momentum carefully. If it doesn't turn up within 5 days, watch out! Consider tightening stops or exiting the trade and waiting for the next setup or trigger.

> **CAUTION:** *The first setup at a new lower low may not be the best setup to buy. Waiting for a rally attempt and pullback towards the past new low can often provide a higher probability entry opportunity. The reason is that after a rally attempt, sellers come back in and force prices down towards the past lower low.*
>
> *If Buyers (Institutions) are going to support the new rally attempt, they will step in on this test towards the lower low. If Buyers fail to step in, it tells Traders that more downside can be expected. The past lower low will probably not hold!*

Triggers 2 and 3 provide a bit more information and confirmation for traders who are more cautious or who don't have as much time to manage trades and re-enter after a stop-out—an important habit if the market hits your trigger twice.

The first three triggers are most often found after longer pullbacks or bearish trends. Option 4 is typically what I use for adding to winning positions, or taking additional trades when the market is up and doesn't have many opportunities for the first three triggers.

You'll find a cheat sheet to download on the book's bonus page AutoPilotTraders.com/Print-Resources. Coupon code PRINT100.

Looking for Setups

If momentum is at or below the oversold extreme (-42) or pulling back, you should be looking for areas of potential support. Look to the left. If you're seeing prices come down toward a support area, you should be anticipating a trade. With those two pieces in place, a desirable price point for your trade trap should be evident with a little practice.

In general, I place my trade traps very close to the price area that initiates my trigger. For example, if I define an area of support at $50, I will trigger my entry order just 10-20 cents above that level. The same applies to the other triggers, such as moving averages or the midpoint of large candles. There are enough opportunities available where that level of precision will work that I don't feel the need to chase stocks as they go higher.

Do I miss some opportunities by being that precise? Yes.

But I keep my risk small and defined on every trade.

We'll get more into the mechanics of exactly how to set those trade traps in later chapters. The important point for now is that you understand and recognize the few simple pictures that fit our PEP Routine analysis.

Why It's Worth Waiting

Many trade systems are based on price action, and some even focus on candles. These provide some high-probability setups that are valuable.

But momentum is the ingredient that makes the real difference.

It's the clue that minimizes buying at support and watching the stock go sideways. It increases the odds of rapid growth when combined with the other two signals.

A quick review: With the PEP Routine, the chart is telling me I'm ready to trade (searching for my trigger) when I see:

1. Price near a support zone
2. Confirmed reversal candlesticks
3. Momentum (TSI) in one of our three conditions: oversold, divergent, or at its own support areas.

⊢₊╬⊦╦

A critical part of training when I deployed with my first Squadron, VA-25, was learning to recognize threat aircraft, ships, and submarines. We would spend hours memorizing photos and silhouettes of these potential dangers. While learning to recognize price patterns is not a matter of physical life or death, it could mean the difference between the life or death of your trading capital.

The good news – traders can be extremely successful if they focus and learn a single setup. The next chapter will present some simplified pictures of our PEP Routine Setup using price patterns that reveal our Value Action Zone.

Each of the elements—Price Action, Momentum, and Trigger—gives a clue that a setup is happening. When the clues begin to converge in the same area, it increases our confidence in the setup and shows us exactly where to set our trade trap to trigger an entry.

Learning to wait for the convergence of clues will increase the probability of a solid trade trigger. Remember, not all trade triggers result in a profitable trade, but waiting for the recognizable setup will provide a winning edge if the mechanical rules are followed consistently.

⊢₊╬⊦╦

THE IMPORTANCE OF WAITING: *Most traders lose money because they fail to wait for a predefined proper mechanical setup! They over-anticipate and enter prematurely before seeing a confirmed convergence of price, momentum and trigger. I've been guilty of impatience myself, entering when it "looks like" a momentum indicator "might" be turning. That anticipation ends with losses.*

Waiting for the clues adds to the weight of evidence that a high probability trade can be planned. Waiting is a discipline that takes practice and time to develop.

Most traders need to see and trade the setup at least 50 to 200 times. You can practice execution and patience without the losses by using a simulation tool like paper trading or the On Demand feature of the ThinkorSwim trading platform. Just like flying, a little time in the simulator will prevent crashing and burning because of rookie mistakes.

Previously, we talked about chart patterns as "predictable" because they relied on human nature and had a statistically significant repeating outcome.

When we read charts, we're looking for clues that one of those patterns has, or might be, forming again. The more of our clues converge at the same time around a targeted area of the chart, the more confidence we have that it's an appropriate area to take action according to our rules.

Reading charts is simply recognizing the convergence of clues that reveal our pattern and our ideal place to take action. Just like runway lights help a pilot set up for a nighttime landing, or evidence of a mouse telling you where to intervene, the convergence of clues shows you where there is a high potential for profit.

When you see the clues come together, decide where you want to place your traps.

Defining an Edge

When a set of similar conditions has resulted in a 60-65% chance of profitability in the past, it's considered a high-probability setup.

The convergence of clues for the Precision Entry Point Routine fits comfortably within that range.

This is the definition of a market edge.

Learning to interpret the Convergence of Clues when trading is probably the most important element of reducing trading risk and increasing trade success probability. Much like a mathematical equation with multiple variables, as values are assigned to each variable, the equation becomes easier to solve and with greater accuracy!

As clues converge, dots start connecting that lead a trader to make a higher probability decision regarding entering or exiting a trade. The more clues that point to a certain action, the better.

Often, we do not know why price reacts at a specific VAZ—it might be news or crowd behavior—but we can see the Convergence of Clues and prepare with a higher level of certainty for a specific outcome because that outcome has happened more often than not in the past. Again, it doesn't happen every time, but it does happen all the time.

However, if our anticipated outcome does not happen *this* time, other rules kick in to mitigate damage and reduce risk. That's where our next set of rules come into play. But first, let's look at further examples of the 3-Step Precision Entry Points Setup and the potential variations it may present.

⊢+⊕⊦⊕

Review:

Precision Entry Point Routine
The chart is telling us to look for a trade trigger when we see a convergence of:
1. Price at a support zone (look to the left to find them).
2. Reversal candlestick patterns in that support zone (confirmation preferred).
3. Momentum (TSI) turning up from one of three conditions: oversold, bullish divergence, or at one of its support areas.

Triggers
Depending on your tolerance for risk and whipsaw, the triggers to place an order to open a trade are:
1. Early: With a confirmed candlestick pattern at support if momentum is slowing but hasn't yet turned up.
2. Momentum Turn: Near support, after the momentum has crossed up from oversold.
3. Close Above 8-Day: After momentum has turned up and the price closes above the 8-day EMA, with the order close to the 8-day.
4. Flags in Existing Uptrend: When the 3 chart signals appear in short-term pullbacks (flags) during an uptrend, use bounces off the 8, 20, or 50-day moving averages, or drawn trend lines.

Also, these two special cases:
A. Large Bullish Candles: When using Trigger 3, if the close above the 8 is on a large bullish candle, use either the 8-day or the midpoint on the candle for your entry.

B.   Gap Higher: If a flag/pullback ends with a small body candle (doji) and gaps higher, follow Trigger 4.

Patience is a virtue, and waiting for the convergence of the PEP signals is good for your account and your psyche.

CHAPTER TEN

CONVERGENCE SCENARIOS

Back in 1871, a Prussian officer said something that has been paraphrased down to the adage: "No plan survives first contact with the enemy." Even Mike Tyson expressed the same idea when he reportedly said, "Everybody has a plan until they get punched in the mouth!" And I've heard being hit by Mike Tyson made you feel like your brains would pop out of your head.

The idea holds in trading. There will be times when the market does a head-fake and hits you. Your job is to hold onto your brains.

The 3-Step PEP Routine reveals an area to set a trade trap, but the market will show it to you in different ways that can fool you. Like a pilot who is learning to land a plane, you don't just see the runway lights and point the nose at the ground. You have to practice recognizing both the signals and the conditions—and then practice executing your plan under different scenarios.

Later, we'll show you how to do that without the risk of losing any money.

But this chapter shares multiple chart conditions where you'll see the PEP Routine Setup and how your perception might shift when you see them.

Remember, we're looking for clues intersecting at Value Action Zones. When we first recognize that it's happening, it may be too early to act. This means we must have a specific proven plan for what steps to take when clues start converging—then find that VAZ where you will decide to place your trade trap.

Let's review the variables I'm observing while planning a potential trade set up:

- Is Price Action nearing support or resistance?
- Is there a Reversal Candle Pattern?
- TSI Crossing up?

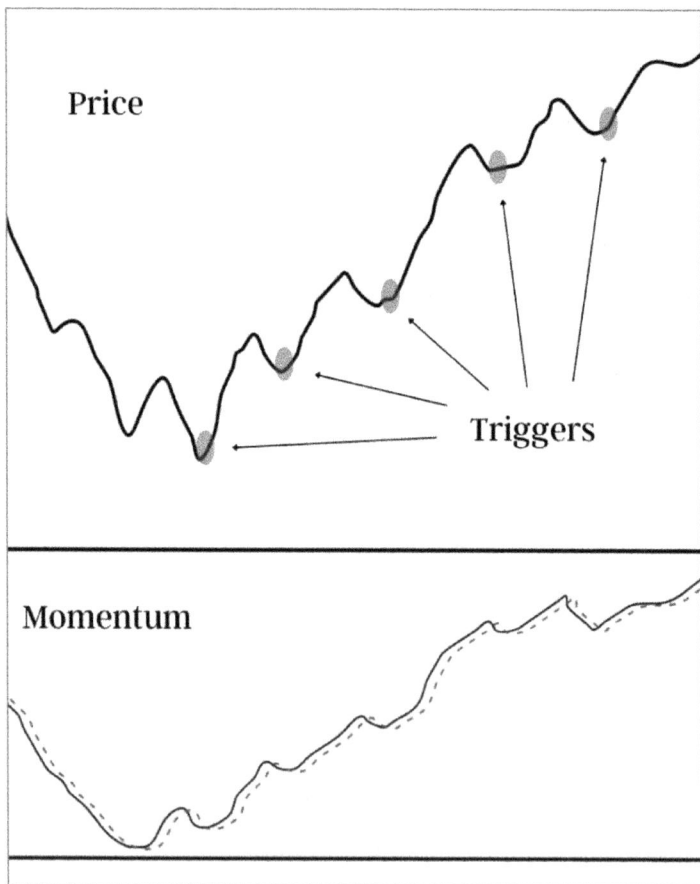

After years of trying to follow dozens of setup options, my eye can easily pick up variations to our combinations of clues that may show up in different charts. I want to give you some examples so you can "borrow" my experience.

Just as familiar people or places can look different under different conditions, so can the pattern. We recognize people in different clothes or venues, and we can train our brains to recognize the patterns under varied market pictures, too.

The PEP Routine Setup doesn't change, but sometimes the chart is obvious when searching for my VAZs, while other times, the picture gets muddied.

And being on the "hard right edge" of the chart always adds some mud. So, let's look at good and bad examples to see what can happen.

NOTE: In each of these examples, the solid line closest to the price is the 8-day Moving Average, the dotted line that lags price somewhat is the 50-day MA, and the dotted line that moves very little and may not even be close to the price is the 200-day MA.

Analog Devices - ADI

ADI went through a relatively sideways trend for about a year. Notice, there are still excellent trading opportunities during that time. Some are better than others.

Observation Points:

    A. Bullish Harami reversal pattern, but no defined support. Oversold momentum has slowed. Taking this is an aggressive Trigger 1.

    B. Testing support from point A. The large candle recovering support is positive. TSI shows divergence. The midpoint of the large candle is an aggressive Trigger 2. For confirmation, wait for the close above the 8-day (Trigger 3).

C. Testing mild support of the gap up from point B. TSI oversold and turning up, but no specific candles. Aggressive Trigger 1.

D. Retesting stronger support with candle Engulfing Pattern. TSI divergent and turning up. Trigger 2 entry possible if very close to support.

E. Final test of support with very large Engulfing Pattern. TSI even more divergent. Trigger 2 possible using "hidden support" in middle of large candle. Turns out, it was a waiting game.

F. Gap up after another test of support. TSI crossing up above 0 level resistance. Attempt to enter on Trigger 3 over the following days.

Setup Examples – ADI

In this case, the weekly chart might have influenced whether any of those trades was right for you.

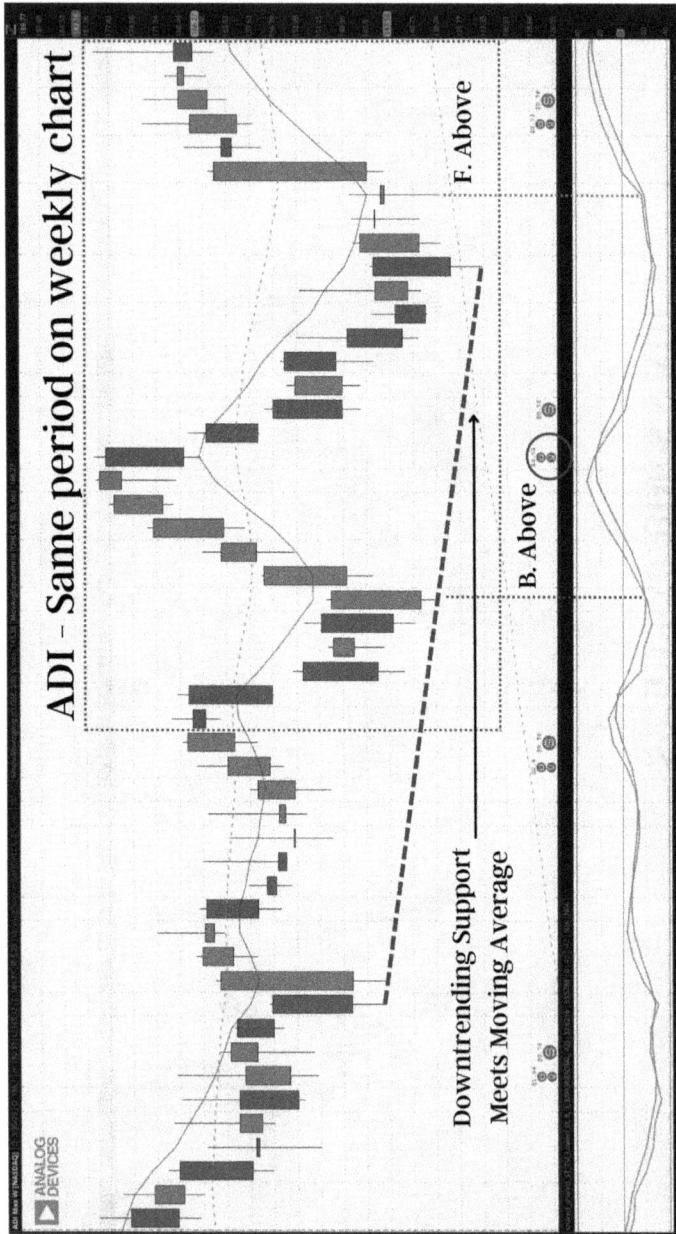

ADI – Same period on weekly chart

The blue box shows the same period as the daily chart above. Notice that after point B, you could have drawn the downtrending support line that eventually intersects with the 200-week moving average (dotted pink line). It looks like the rally failed because of a bad earning event (blue circle). But we would have had more information about support at the ultimate low and the retest at point F by looking at the weekly chart. Would that have made you more or less confident in making a trade?

⊢₊♦⧾♊

Nvidia - NVDA

NVDA does a controlled pullback toward the 200-day moving average before launching in a new uptrend.

Observation Points:

    A. TSI is oversold and turning, but we have no support or candles. This is not a complete setup. Once we get a close above the 8-day, we're up against resistance at the 50-day (yellow dotted line). Not a great Reward:Risk profile.

    B. Multiple tests of the 200-day average (pink dotted line). A couple potential inverted hammers, followed by a hammer with the same bottom. TSI is nicely divergent and turning up from oversold. This is a confident Trigger 1.

    C. A shallow flag (see last chapter) that lingers near the 8-day. As momentum turns, you could look for Trigger 4 at several points with a stop just under the swing low. The large candle at the blue line confirms the new move, but it runs away from you pretty quick. Consider the R:R of entering near the midpoint.

D. Flag to the 50-day. TSI turning at the -20 support. A possible Trigger 4, but with earnings within the week, I might be cautious about a trade.

E. Another flag, but a little sloppy. TSI hovering around the 0 line for support. Without any candles, this is a harder trade. You might look at something after closing back above the 8-day, like a hybrid between Triggers 3 & 4. Without any visible support the close above the 8-day would be a valid trigger.

Setup Examples – NVDA

Nasdaq 100 ETF - QQQ

The Nasdaq has several intermediate trends in this chart. You can probably find several other potential entry points that I didn't highlight in this chart.

Observation Points:

A. V-bottom on price and momentum with no candlesticks. The large green candle closing above the 8-day leaves us looking for Trigger 3, which we get a few days later.

B. Sharp flag pullback to the 50-day and support at the bottom of a gap with a Piercing Line candlestick pattern. TSI slows at the -20 support area with the candle pattern. I'd be confident in Trigger 4 (existing uptrend) here for a short-term trade.

C. Return to support at point A, but no clear candlestick patterns. Momentum is turning up. Large candles put us distant from support, so this does not fit the parameters for Trigger 1. Aggressive traders might get into a position between C and D but would likely be stopped out quickly.

D. A fair Hammer candle, but momentum is dropping, and support at the bottom is untested. Momentum is divergent and near the oversold line, which can be support. Two following candles test that support, but TSI doesn't turn up until the close above the 8-day. Looking for Trigger 3 after that.

E. Clean-looking flag to the moving average cluster and support of a previous swing high (look left). TSI has pulled back to support at +20. However, the sloppy, wide candle at the blue line makes entry challenging. Looking for Trigger 4, which does not happen for over a week. My order would have canceled before filling, and then we're right against resistance at the 200-day moving average.

F. Testing old support. TSI oversold with a gentle turning. Engulfing pattern. This looks like a clean Trigger 1. That 200-day still acts as resistance, which may have muffled this trade. But you get a second bite about two weeks later with a support test and a Hammer.

G. Another V-bottom on price. But TSI gets a double bounce. The gap up and close above the 8-day opens up the possibility for Trigger 3, as long as you're cautious about that overhead resistance.

H. Very similar to point B. Pullback to the 50-day with an Engulfing Pattern. TSI bouncing at -20 again. I'd look at Trigger 4, with my trap set around the middle of the large candle or the 50-day.

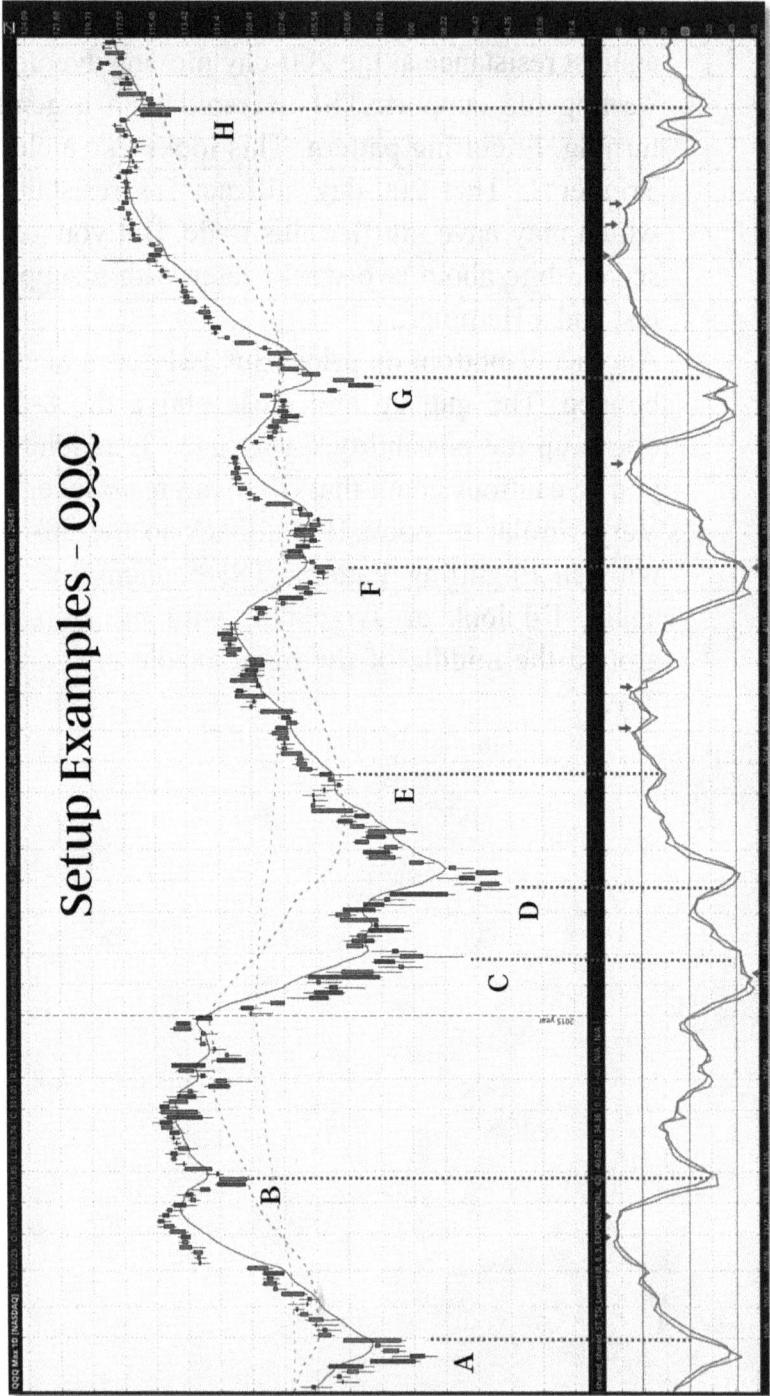

Setup Examples - QQQ

Direxion Daily S&P Oil & Gas Explorers & Producers Bullish 3X ETF- GUSH

This is one of the 3x leveraged ETFs that I love to trade. The advantage of the leveraged entity over the regular sector or index ETF is that you get similar signals, but the moves are enhanced. It can be tough to get an initial 10% move for my first target (next chapter) with the regular index ETFs. It's easy with these leveraged options.

Observation Points:

A. A beautiful Harami pattern at support. TSI is slowing near -20 support. The slope on the 50-day average tells me that this has been in an uptrend, so this is Trigger 4.

B. A Bullish Engulfing pattern after a flag to the 50-day. TSI is lower than previously but turning up. This looks like Trigger 4 again. But the signal quickly turns back around. Negative divergence on the TSI at the previous peak and a sharper pullback might have been a warning, but not enough to say it's not a valid signal. Probably a small gain.

C. Retesting a former high with a Piercing Line. TSI has gone flat while the price continued down (almost divergence). Trigger 1 is valid at the candle's midpoint. For confirmation, wait for Trigger 3.

D. Another flag to the 50-day. TSI resting near +20. I would consider Trigger 4.

E. Not much change, but the 2 candles that almost form an Engulfing Pattern with TSI turning from support again makes me open to Trigger 4. You might not get the entry with the gap a few days later.

F. Mid-length pullback almost to support. TSI over-sold and turning. No candles. This is an incomplete Setup. No go. Gap up makes an entry challenging.

G. Looks like a second chance. Near 200-day average, but no candlestick patterns. TSI has continued up. It might be appropriate to consider Trigger 3 with a close above the 8-day, but with caution. It's easy to see a downtrending resistance line along the previous tops. Along with the rising support level, this looks like a classic triangle pattern forming. It's not something I commonly use to trade, but see how the price gets squeezed down to a point. Once it breaks up or down, it's usually a fast move.

H. After the breakdown from G, we're back in the range of old support. The gap down below support is followed by a gap up that recovers it. This creates a v-bottom in price and momentum. The support was breached, but buyers returned with extreme energy. Trigger 3 is a viable option, though I would be watching resistance levels overhead carefully.

I. A rough flag tests the 50 and 200-day moving averages with indecision candles and TSI in a support region. This third test of the 200-day since the low at point H is positive. I might consider a small trade here as Trigger 4, or wait for the close above 8-day and look for Trigger 3.

J. Price has been tracking in a sideways range just above the old highs. TSI is falling while it looks like support is holding. With a momentum turn near the 0 line, I might consider Trigger 4 here if I can buy right off support, but my first target to take profits would be the overhead resistance. It may not meet our R:R needs.

Setup Examples – GUSH

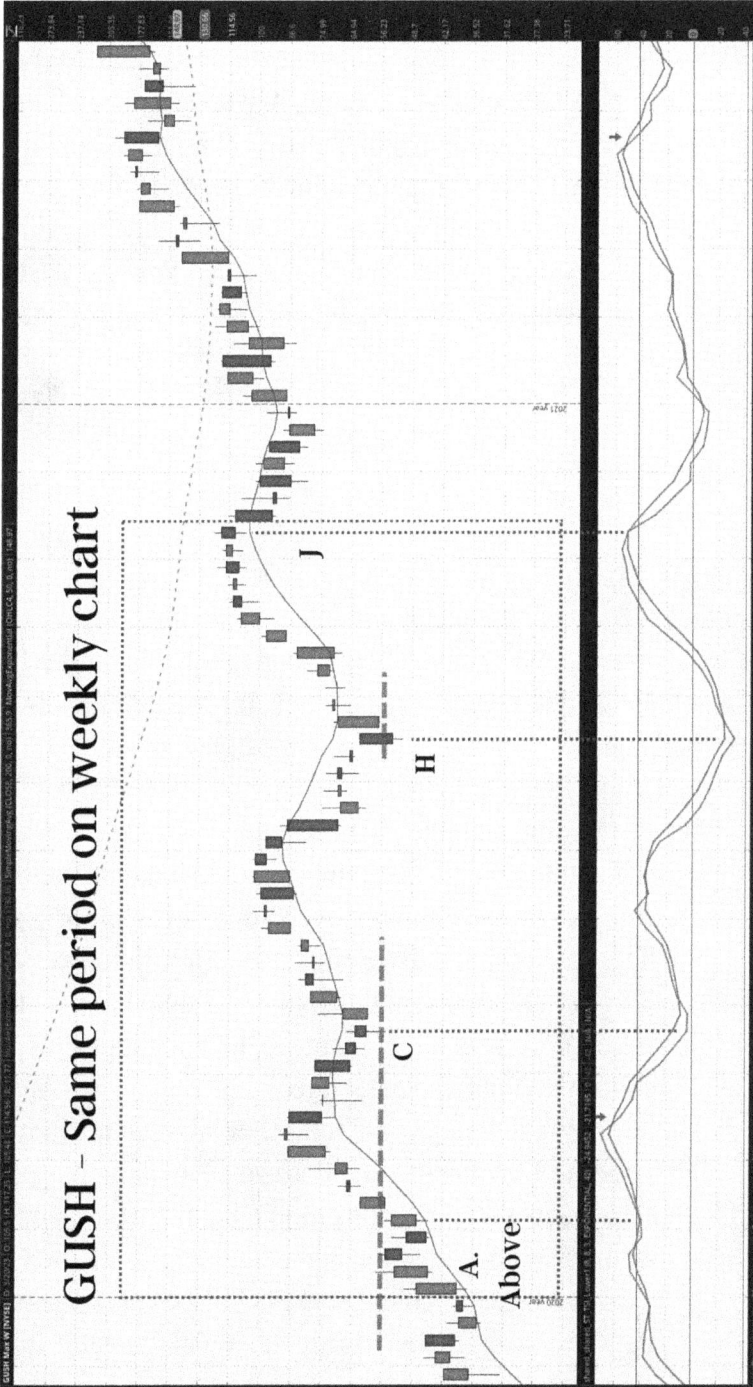

GUSH – Same period on weekly chart

The weekly chart of the same period adds a little more color to the previous example. Point A was definitely a continuation move, with TSI high. Point C was a bounce near the weekly 0 line, a solid trade option. Point H shows that the test of old support had a more significant turning on the weekly chart from a lower low. While the weekly TSI at Point J shows a bearish crossing that deserves caution before jumping in.

Russell 2000 ETF - IWM

The Russell 2000 is one of my favorite indices, and while IWM can be great to trade, I usually prefer the extra leverage from the 3x ETFs

Observation Points:

    A. A Hammer shape at the bottom of a flag, though we usually like to see the hammer head at the bottom. This one shows several hits on support, and TSI has positive divergence. A slightly aggressive Trigger 1 trade or waiting for Trigger 3. In this case, there was also a Trigger 4 opportunity off the 50-day a couple weeks later.

    B. Within a few days of each other, we see a Piercing Line and an Engulfing Pattern in a wide or loose flag. However, it's bottom is a bit far from support at the 50-Day. It might be hitting a shorter moving average like the 20 or 34-day. TSI hovering around 0. Ultimately, the setup fails as it returns to stronger support at C.

C. Indecision candle at old highs shows strong support. TSI slows around -20. Without better candles, our best chance here is Trigger 3, on or after the blue line.

D. Close enough to a Bullish Engulfing recovering the 50-day. TSI bouncing from the -42 line. Short-lived Trigger 4. On the 3x ETF, it may have been worth it.

E. A second chance with positive divergence on TSI. Most likely a Trigger 3 on the close above the 8-day.

F. Flag to the 50-day with a gap up and close above the 8-day. TSI bouncing from -20 support. Trigger 3 & 4 hybrid.

G. Another flag to the 50-day. Piercing Line type pattern with TSI turning from around -20. Trigger 4. Look for hidden support around the midpoint of the large candles for your precise entry.

H. Harami pattern at the 50 after another flag. TSI is still falling, but near previous support. Being right at price support puts my stop extremely close, so I'm not risking much to take this as Trigger 4, or you could wait for confirmation with a close above the 8-day (Trigger 3)

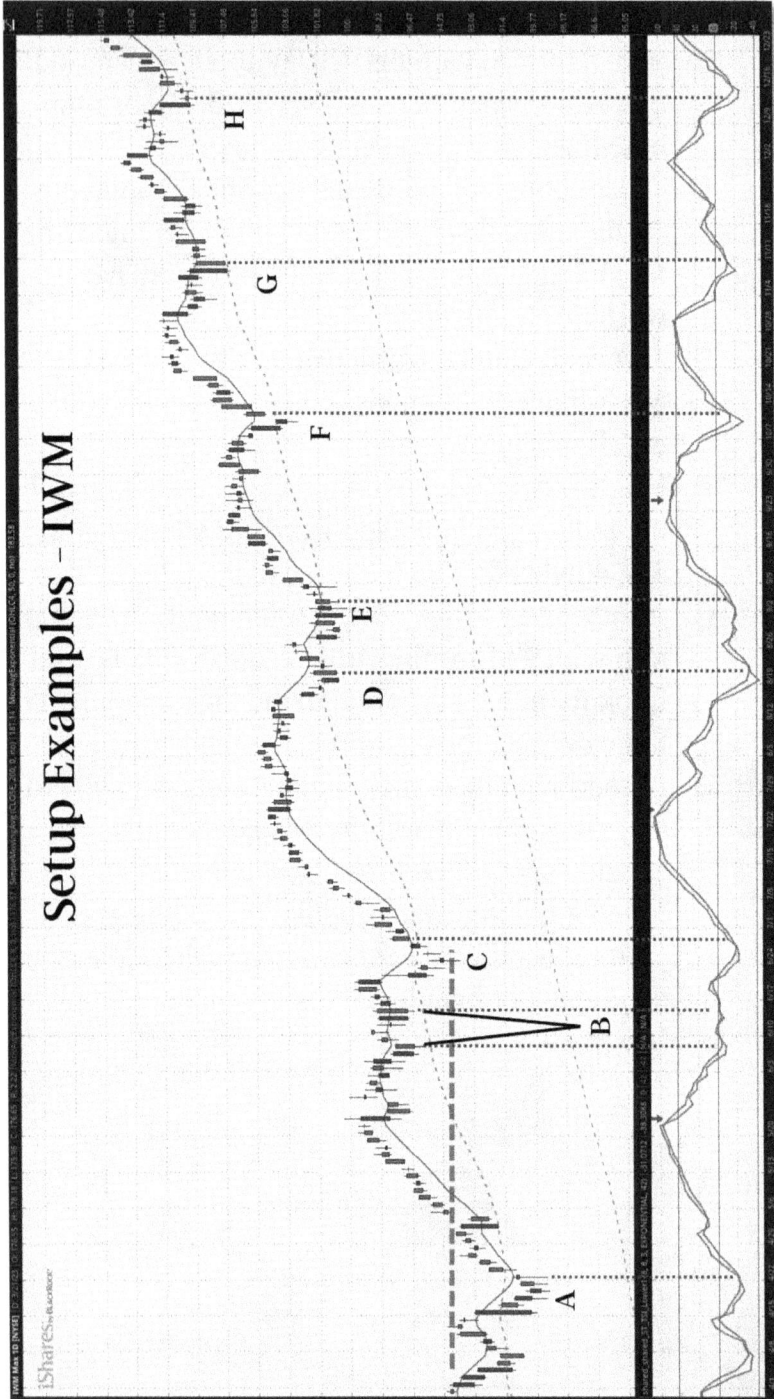

Setup Examples – IWM

We could fill books with example charts like this (Bill ONeil did). I hope that this reinforces the hand-drawn concept at the beginning of this chapter and the concept of waiting for Price, Momentum, and Trigger to make your entry.

Practice:

- Spend time with your favorite chart and practice just seeing examples of the Precision Entry Points Setup and Triggers.
- Think about where you might set your trade trap and why. No need to write anything down yet. This is just about seeing the pattern.
- If you find it challenging, review this chapter and the last one. Walk through the process with one TSI condition, like oversold.
  - Find support areas.
  - Look for candlestick patterns (see appendix)
  - Find potential triggers 1-4
- For advanced practice, try finding examples on the right edge of the chart and clicking forward to see how it plays out.
- Make it a game at first.

CHAPTER ELEVEN

PILLAR 3 – WHEN, WHERE, AND HOW TO EXIT

Nothing happens until you pull the trigger and buy a position. Many traders get so caught up in exactly where they *"should"* buy that they lose sight of something more important.

Where you buy only determines your risk—the amount you might lose on the trade.

Where you sell determines your profit.

Your buy point has an effect on your profit potential, yes, but potential is not a guarantee.

You can estimate areas where a stock price *might* go in the near future—and you want to take trades with a higher probability of moving toward those targets with momentum, as in the last section—but it's never a sure thing.

It's not a profit until you actually sell. That's why "where to exit" is the realm of intense emotions like regret and euphoria, greed and fear—any of which can cause you to make stupid decisions.

Don't make stupid decisions.

Be a wise trader and have a decisive plan *before* you enter your buy order!

Remember, trading and investing is about making decisions that are compromises. When, Where and How you exit a trade is about making probability-based decisions that are compromises. Accepting these compromises can challenge some traders from a mindset and psychological perspective.

But when you decide *what* you're going to do <u>before your money is at risk</u>, you'll make more profitable decisions and you'll have more peace in your trading career.

This chapter covers several equally important places to close out your trades. We'll look at the worst case, the average case, and the best case, along with contingency plans for unusual situations.

Learn to Cover Your Assets

First, let's consider the catastrophic stop loss. This is your first compromise choice. The mental compromise is this: sometimes good setups fail—therefore, when I set stops, I'm managing my risk so that surprises never blow up my account or ruin my ability to make good decisions.

Many traders scoff at mechanical stops and use a "mental stop" where they *say* they will take the hit and exit a position at a loss. Too many times, the price drops below that mental stop, and you start to create the opposite justification to what was just mentioned… "It's not a loss until you sell," these traders-in-trouble say. They *hope* the position will come back so they can get out at break even, but if the price continues to drop, it only increases the pain, leading to further bad choices.

Hope isn't a strategy.

It's one thing to have a plan for exiting with a minimal loss. It's another thing to ensure that your plan gets executed. I teach that you should always set a mechanical stop to protect your capital. Without capital to invest, your trading is dead in the water.

So set stops and be grateful for the convenience of managing your risk on autopilot. Ideally, I like to include my stop loss order linked to my entry order. I'll explain exactly how to do that in part three. For now, we're considering where to place your stop.

The first method for choosing where to place stops is based on observable chart patterns. Once you know the three-step setup and trigger, you'll know where the price "shouldn't go" for you to stay in the trade. This no-go zone is another action zone, usually support, and I often place my stop loss just below that zone. When I say just below, I mean 10-50 cents below, depending on how volatile the price has been recently. This typically puts my stop loss order 3-5% below my entry price.

Remember, support can be horizontal, diagonal, or dynamic. It might be the bottom of a candlestick pattern or a moving average. The more examples you study, the easier it is to see.

The second method is simpler, but I typically only use it when the no-go action zone is a bit too far away for my risk profile. This is my catastrophic stop loss, the maximum I'm ever willing to lose on a given trade. The catastrophic stop loss should be between 5-7% below my entry price.

One of the often-overlooked considerations connected to a stop loss is using it to project profits based on a prudent Reward:Risk Ratio. Consistent traders typically set a Reward:Risk of 2 or 3 for every trade. This means that for every dollar risked, they expect a two- or three-dollar reward. Translating to percentages, a 3:1 Reward:Risk would mean the profit target covering a 5% stop loss would be 15%. A

7% stop translates to a profit target of 21% with the same 3:1 R:R ratio.

Fifteen to twenty-one percent is usually within my measured target for the PEP Routine Setup and the types of entities I trade. That is the technical reason why I put my catastrophic stop loss at 5-7 percent. It also happens to be the amount of loss I can live with psychologically on a given trade. Much more and my emotions lead me toward bad decisions.

You might be able to handle more. Just know that any adjustment will change your parameters and might not work with the PEP Routine Setup if you modify the R:R ratio.

The important part is that you protect capital with a mechanical stop—whether measured or catastrophic. Pick one that's right for your situation.

Why take profits off the table?

Capital protection with stops is only half the equation. You can maintain wealth by never losing money, but you can't grow wealth without profit. That is, of course, not factoring in the wealth-eroding force of inflation. Even maintenance needs some growth.

For success in trading, you must learn how to take profit and protect it!

I know that this would appear to be obvious, but many traders have a "deer in the headlights" experience when it comes to taking profits. Because profit-taking is not included in their written trading plan, they will watch with glee as prices move up 5%, 10%, 20%, or higher and then stare in confusion as price action reverses and falls back toward their buy point.

The trader holds on to the position until it is half the gain it was, or even a loss—the devastating result of lacking a complete plan! I believe it is equally important, if not more important, to learn how to take profits and protect existing gains than to simply limit losses. Developing this skill helps a trader make profit-taking a habit!

Mechanical Targets

Mechanical Profit Targets are an excellent way to start. A simple approach is to divide a new position into three parts. (I'll share my preferred ratio in a later chapter.) Establish Profit Targets at 7-10% (PT1), 17-25% (PT2), and over 30% (PT3), respectively. Based on where I set my maximum stop loss, this offers that 2-3 Reward:Risk ratio we want. If I measure out a closer stop, it only improves my R:R.

This method removes worrying about the nuances of technical analysis while you're learning and have money at risk, thus letting you focus on recognizing and executing on the PEP Routine.

By taking profits at established percentage points routinely, a trader will learn how to be a winner!

That'll do a lot for your mental game.

But remember that trading is about making compromises. Taking profits at set percentage points is a compromise. If the price action continues to move higher, you can miss out on larger potential profits. Learn to develop a mindset that lets go of the "could haves" and attached second-guessing emotions! Learn how to win first, then learn the more precise mechanics of measured targets and letting your winners run.

Profit Alternatives Using Measured Targets

While I like to have traders take profits at set percentage points, as described above, there are times when a more technical approach is necessary.

Measured Profit Targets and Trailing Stops are based on observable, objective price action that has taken place in the past or on dynamic support and resistance. I split my trade into three portions again, and as above, assign a Profit Target to each portion.

Two widely used techniques help me take at least partial profits when the chart shows resistance before my normal PT1 at 10%. The first is resistance at past swing highs. The second is Fibonacci extension and retracement levels.

> *Note: As I go through this example, don't forget the "hidden areas" of support or resistance, like the middle of large candles. You may also consider dynamic support, like trendlines you draw on the chart or major moving averages like the 50-day and 200-day, or a bunched up cluster of moving averages.*

Method One: Technical Resistance from Swing Highs

The first technique is applicable when price action is moving into a new uptrend. Past swing highs on the charts show rally attempts that failed. The reason new upward price action pauses or even reverses at these swing highs is because each of these levels identifies a pocket of sellers. These pockets have traders just waiting for prices to get back to where they bought so that they can get the heck out at breakeven or for a smaller loss.

When past price action identifies a level of technical resistance that is less than my percentage-based target, I must be willing to call an audible and exit early with a lower profit, or protect myself at breakeven. When the price moves into the resistance of a VAZ, a rally attempt may fail prior to hitting the objective of my usual PT1 at 10%. Let's walk through this scenario on a chart. This snapshot of NFLX below (Chart 1) ends on 3/29/21 and provides an excellent example of price action forming a base and getting ready to move into a new uptrend. From the projected entry point, the first swing high is a bit over 6% away, which is less than my desired 10% (PT1).

While I don't want to place an exit order at the first swing high, I do want to monitor price action as it approaches this level of resistance. Additionally, if a trader thought that the price would turn against them hard, then selling part of the position when the swing high is hit would be another approach. If price action stalls, falls, and fails to get through this level, I want to tighten stops to at least breakeven.

Price action shown on Chart 2 clearly shows that as prices rose, enough sellers were waiting at the first swing high to stop the upward momentum. The stalling nature of this price action is enough to at least tighten stops to breakeven. The Hanging Man bearish reversal signal also gives credence to tightening stops but not necessarily closing the position.

In Chart 3, we see that patience pays off. Following the Hanging Man candlestick, price action broke through this swing high level. Notice that in the following days, old resistance becomes a new support zone. This eventually acts as the springboard to hit Profit Target 1 (PT1) fifteen days after our entry point.

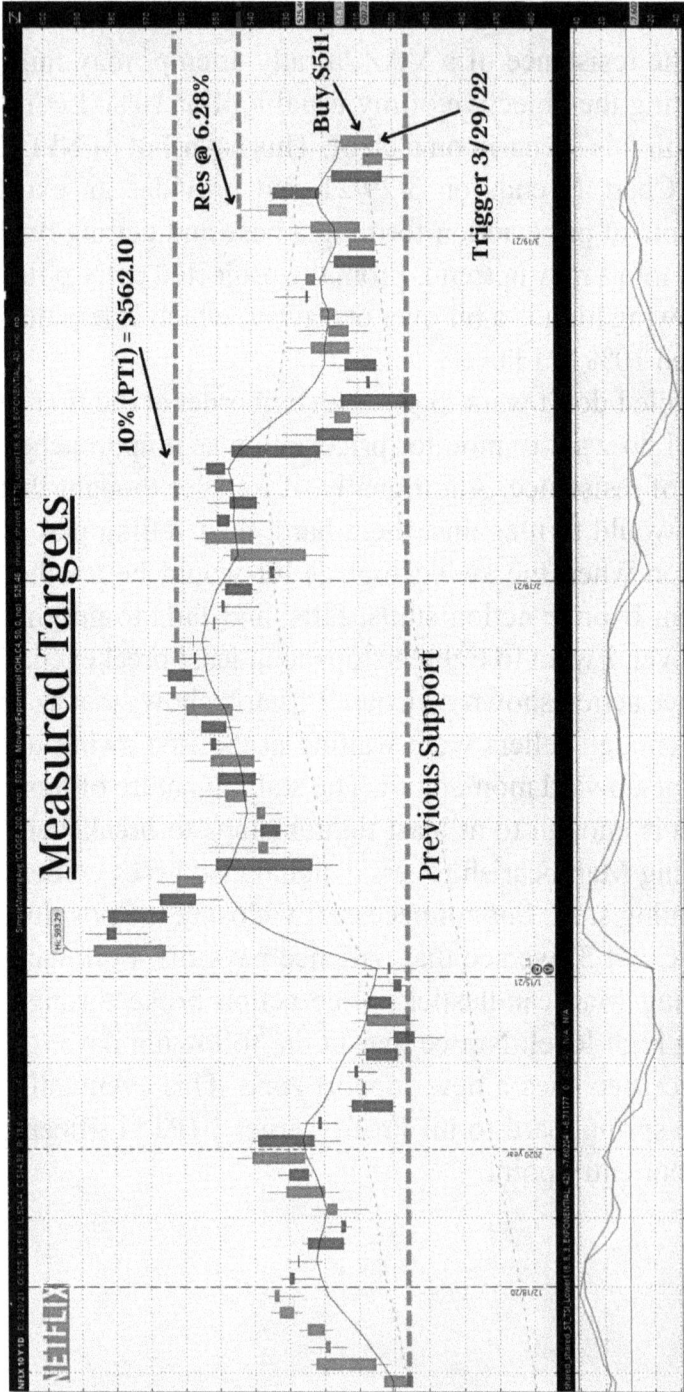

NFLX Chart 1

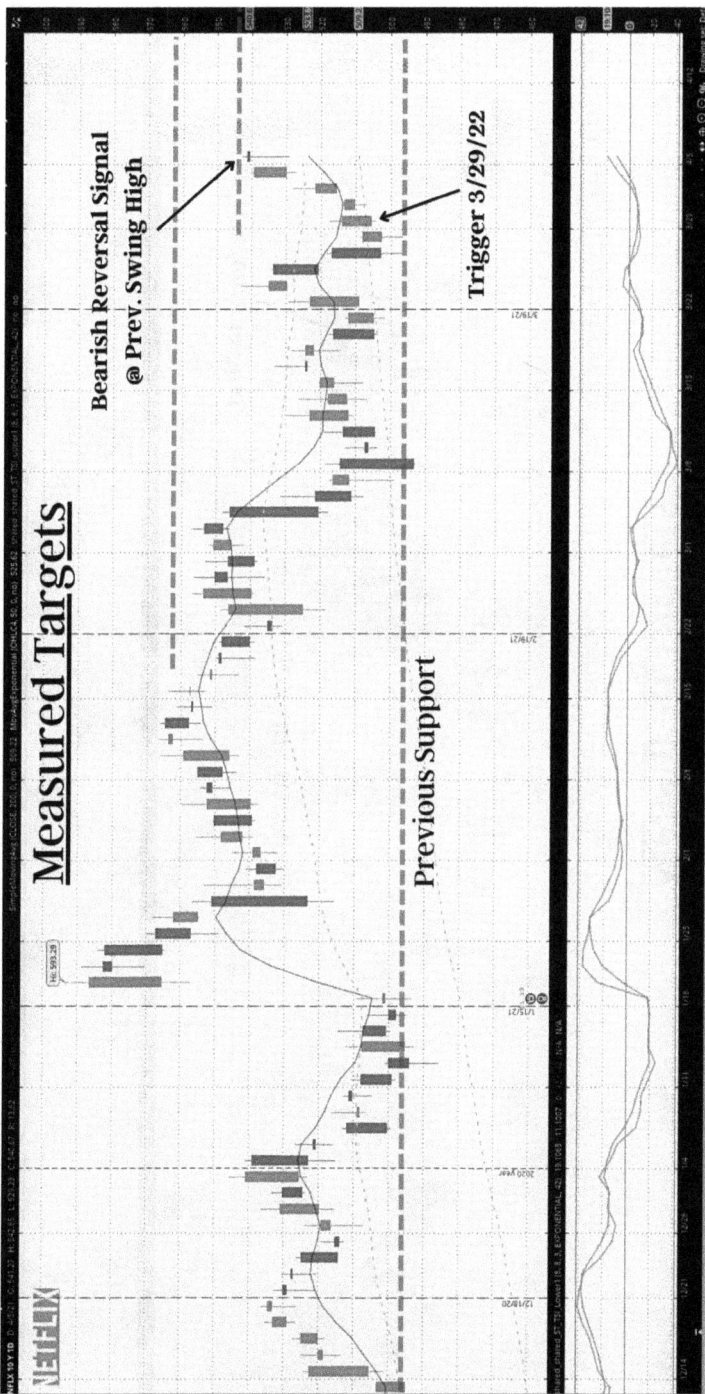

NFLX Chart 2

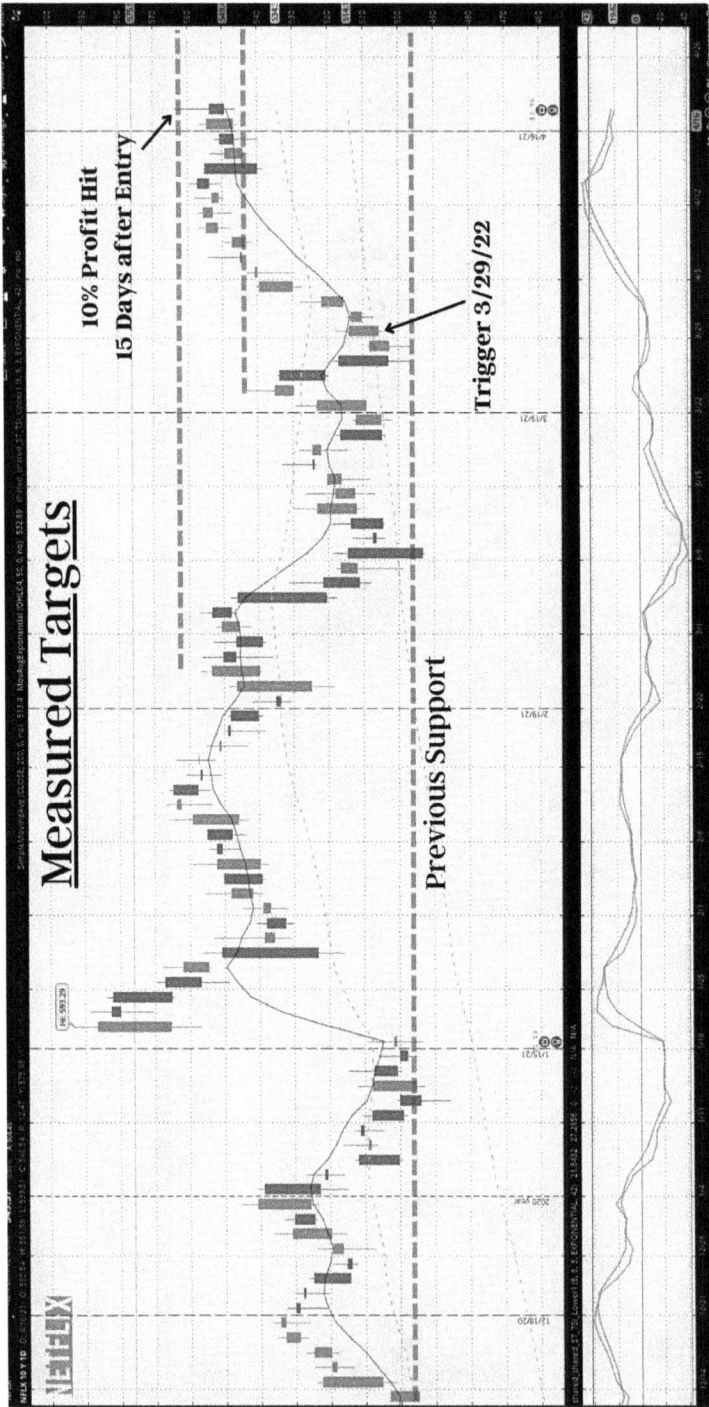

Measured Targets

10% Profit Hit
15 Days after Entry

Trigger 3/29/22

Previous Support

NFLX Chart 3

Method Two: Fibonacci Levels

Fibonacci levels are based on a centuries-old mathematical sequence made popular in Europe in 1202 by a man named Fibonacci. The number sequence has been used in computer algorithms, data science, art, and architectural design since it is closely related to the Golden Ratio. What's surprising is that the sequence also appears frequently in nature, from the growth patterns of certain plants to the population expansion of rabbits, the shell spiral of the nautilus, and even the orbits in our solar system and the patterns in spiral galaxies. These numbers show up everywhere.

Some brilliant technician noticed it also repeats in crowd-based behaviors like stock market trading. Traders have been applying Fibonacci numbers to charts ever since, and I think you'll be a little surprised if you haven't seen them before.

For consistency and to show the overlap between the Technical targets discussed earlier, I'll use NFLX over the same timeframe.

Fibonacci Retracements

On **Fibonacci Retracements**, look for a significant swing move that is a single run.

In this case, I measure from the high on 3/2/22 down to the low on 3/8/22. As often happens, Fibonacci measurements provide additional clues as to where price action may move. On a side note, I'm not sure if it's the "magic of the fibs" or just a self-fulfilling action due to many traders watching the Fibonacci levels. Either way, it doesn't happen every time, but it does happen all the time.

My major Levels of Interest for both **Fibonacci Retracements** and **Fibonacci Extensions** are: 38.2, 50, 61.8, 78.6, 100, 127.2 & 161.8.

It is interesting how Chart 4 below shows the 78% retracement level at almost the same level as the first swing high. So, when technical resistance is supported by a Fibonacci Retracement level, pay attention. This is a significant VAZ!

The same process as defined above for adjusting stops or taking partial profits when price action hits the resistance of the Swing High and Fibonacci Retracement level is appropriate.

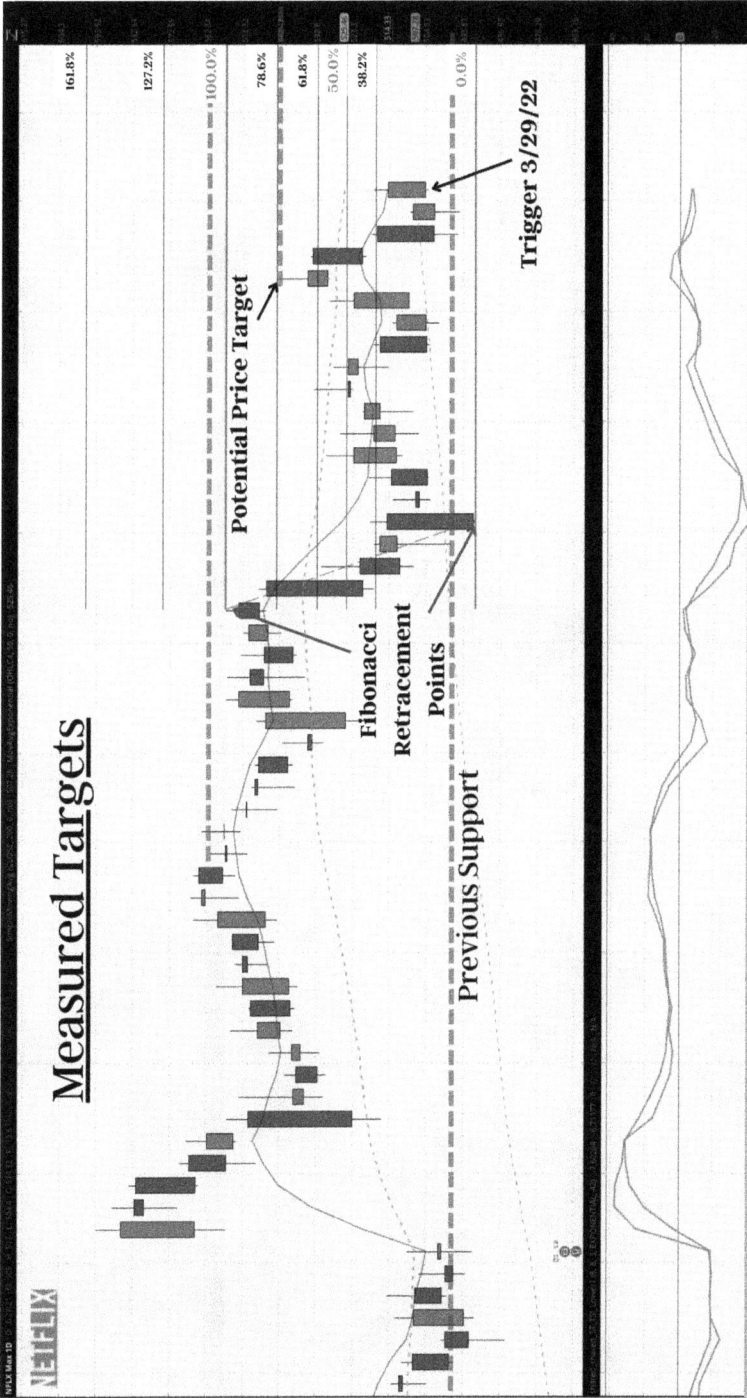

NFLX Chart 4 – Fibonacci Retracement

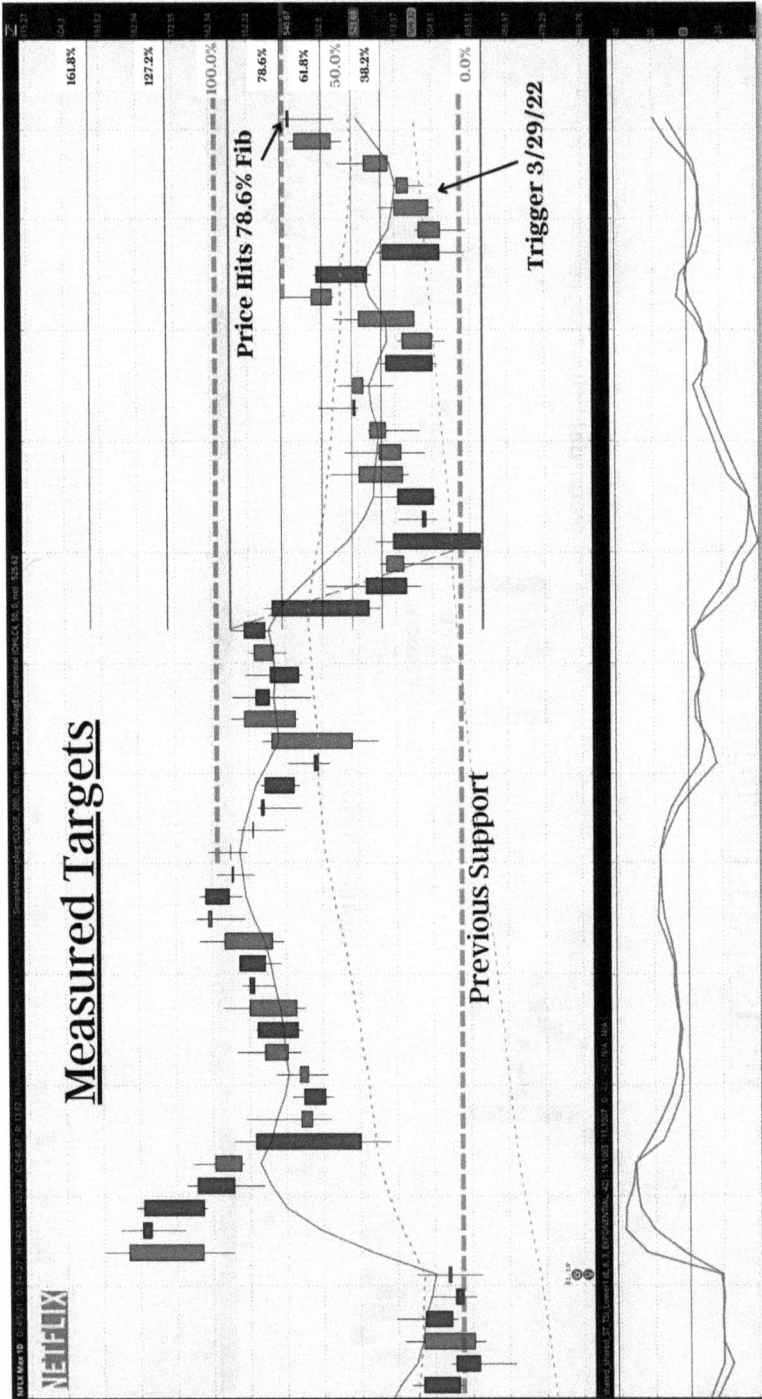

NFLX Chart 5

NFLX Chart 6

As the price moves higher as reflected on Chart 6, above, several clues become visible. Notice how price action stalled and dropped at the 100% retracement. This price pullback provided just enough additional momentum to reach PT1 of 10%, but that 100% Fib level proved too strong for the stock to close above it.

Fibonacci Extensions

For **Fibonacci Extensions**, you'll use two legs of a move as you'll see on the last two charts. For either type of measurement, I generically refer to them as "fibs."

Fib extensions provide an indication of symmetry of price movement and reveal the tendency for price move patterns to repeat . Chart 7 shows an extension from the two-leg pattern just before the rally. When using either retracements or extensions, always look to the left after they are in place to see if they align with past levels of support or resistance. In this case, both 127.2% and 161.8% were significant levels that affected price action. These clues can help you plan your trades before price action occurs by showing you where resistance VAZs might demand more caution.

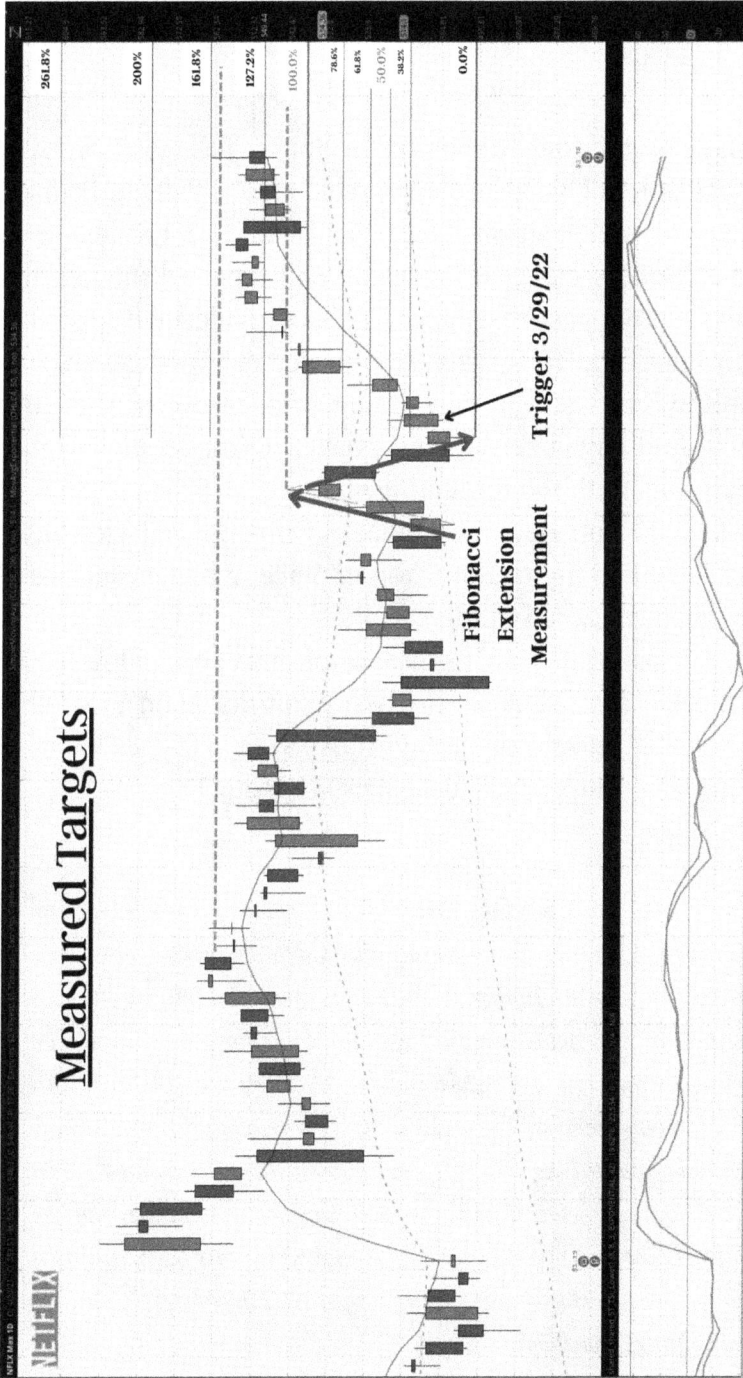

NFLX Chart 7 – Fibonacci Extension

Bonus Observation – Why I don't hold over earnings!

I have a standing rule never to hold a full position over earnings unless I've already achieved a 10% gain and closed out part of the position. Note the Fibonacci Extension in Chart 8. Sellers came in on queue and repelled the attempt to move above past resistance. This coincided with the day of earnings. The following day, prices dropped about 8%. By following a strong rule going into earnings, the 10% profit would have been in your pocket if you decided to ride out earnings with the remaining shares.

I say, "If you decided," because my normal exit rules would have had my trailing stop in place, which would have likely been triggered in this case.

If you would like a full tutorial on how to use Fibonacci levels, here are the links to my two-part tutorial on YouTube.

Tutorial 1: https://youtu.be/9IOA6SJZxW0
Tutorial 2: https://youtu.be/ozmlnYVqtcQ

MOVING AVERAGE DEBATE: *Which type of moving average is best: Simple or Exponential? The camps are divided on whether the Simple Moving Average (SMA) or Exponential Moving Average (EMA) is best. Both have pros and cons. I use the EMA version on moving averages 50 and below and the SMA on the 100 and 200-period moving averages. The major decision point (compromise) is picking something and sticking with it. You will find that some stocks and ETFs will fit one type better than the other. I have found that over time, an entity will sometimes respect the EMA and other times the SMA. It is not worth the effort to change moving average types in order to fit a specific chart during a specific time period.*

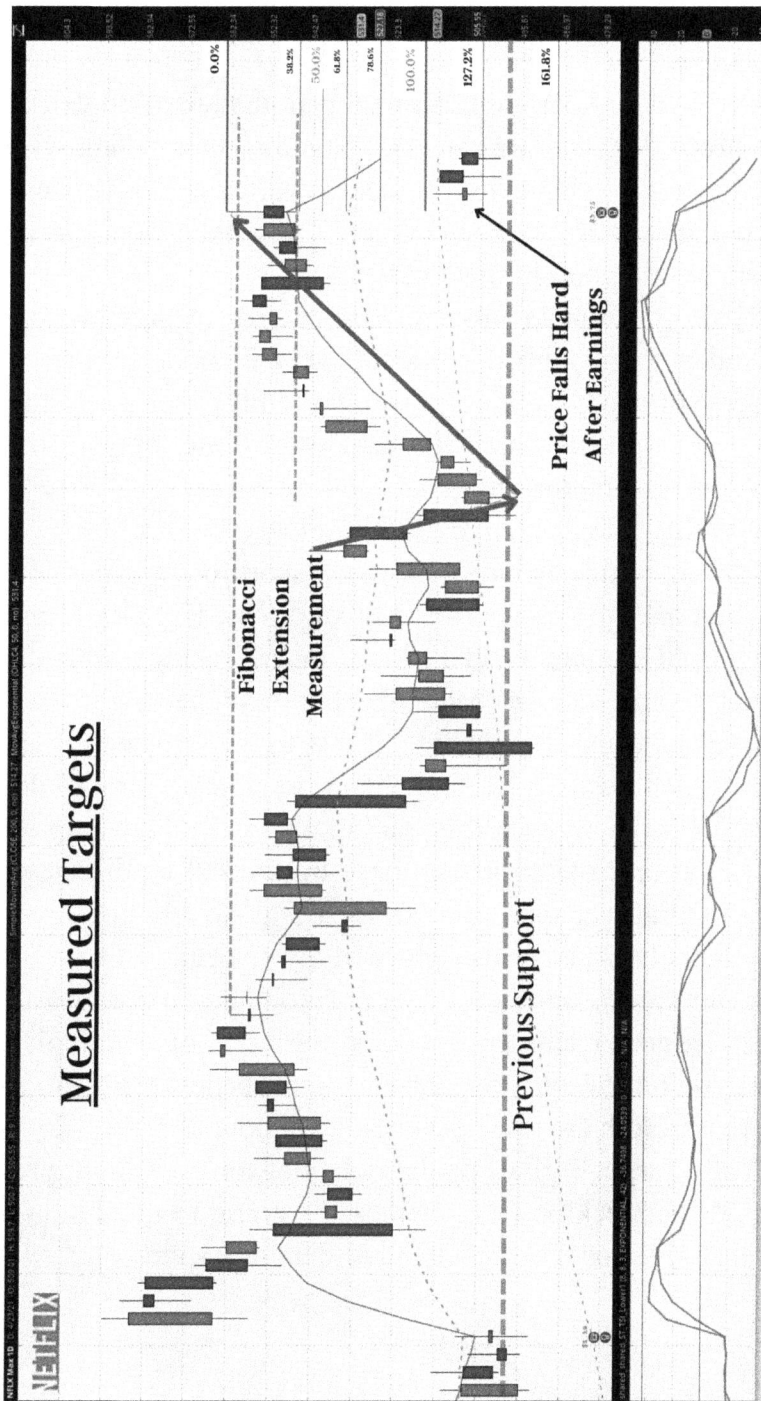

NFLX Chart 8 – Fibonacci Extension after a move.

Splitting up your position

As I'll share later, you can automate the orders to exit at your profit targets. You can even "bundle" them along with the entry order. The technical details will be in a later chapter, but here's the concept that I call either Conditional Orders or "Fire and Forget" trades.

I typically "bundle" my entry order with my stop loss order and all of my profit targets. Every once in a while, a trigger will get you into a position and hit either your stop loss or PT1 on the same day, so I want those orders to be there even if I'm not watching.

Actually, I don't plan on watching!

Nothing brings up emotions like a short round-trip.

When an entry order fills, my stop loss, PT1, PT2, and PT3 are all automated. If I'm still in the position after the market closes, I can go back after hours to check whether I want to make any adjustments. But with the Fire and Forget trades, I don't usually need to change anything. I already decided I'd be happy with this trading plan when I set it up.

The process of setting up these trades will be discussed more in a later chapter. Just know it's given me more freedom than almost any other piece of my system.

As for the reason to split your position into different parts, Profit Targets 1 and 2 get you in the habit of winning! It gives you returns on a regular basis and secures the position from loss. Both are huge psychological boons.

Profit Target 3 gives us the potential for even higher returns if the stock or ETF decides it's going to the moon—and that gives us the chance to build extra wealth.

Letting Winners Run for PT3

Letting Winner's Run is challenging and often it seems like Murphy's Law kicks in when holding long-term. But sometimes, the market gives you a much longer and more profitable run than expected.

Here is a tested approach that has a higher probability of sticking with a stock or ETF for a significant run on the third portion of a position.

After you exit at PT2 (or somewhere around 20%-25% gains)

- Switch to a Weekly or Monthly Chart for exit signals
- Set a Trailing Stop at 12.5% -15% of the current price
- Use Stops 2-3% below swing lows as they appear and when higher than your trailing stop.
- Fire and Forget orders allow you to work these two types of stops to your advantage as the price climbs. This looks like ratcheting your stop higher to secure profits, while allowing for reasonable pullbacks.
- Watch for bearish candlestick reversals and momentum reversals (TSI), especially with negative divergence.
- If you see one of the warning signs above, look for support beneath these reversal signals where you might raise your stop to protect profit.

Yes, stocks sometimes run for 100% gains or more, but not without intermediate and short-term pullbacks that can eat your profits. If a stock is going to pull back more than 15%, I want to protect existing gains and wait for the next setup—not ride the rollercoaster.

Remember, every loss requires a greater gain to get back to even. If you lose 50%, you now need a 100% return to get back to where you started. That puts extra pressure on you to perform, so it's better to keep your losses minimal.

You never know when that moderate pullback will turn into a crash, so protect yourself.

Contingency Exits – What happens if price action doesn't reach Profit Targets?

So, you've planned your trade with a projection of where price action should go if it follows past patterns. But it fails to reach identified price targets. The trade is profitable, but price action is stalling out with momentum weakening.

The simple solution is to let the original exit orders (stops) provide the capital protection as designed. This is a reasonable approach when you're unable to check on the price action—even after hours—for instance, when you're on vacation or don't have internet access.

However, most of us find it prudent to check on positions once per day once money is at risk—even if it's after hours. This check takes just a few moments and can be done on your mobile device with most brokers.

When I'm observing price action at the end of the day or after hours, I look for bearish candlestick reversal signals. If one shows up prior to reaching profit targets, it could be a precursor to an early price reversal.

In order to not jump the gun on adjusting the stop, I want to be in the trade for about 4-5 days and have at least 5% profit before considering modifying the trade. Otherwise, you'll face that frustrating Murphy's Law and pull your stop up before one last test of support.

When those conditions are met, and I see signs that the stock might not reach PT1 as above, I often bring my original stop up to breakeven or change it to a trailing stop of 7.5% of the current price (NOT my entry price).

If my original stop was at 3-5%, then a breakeven stop just preserved trading capital.

If my profit was at 5%, then the trailing stop would have a worst-case exit with a negligible 2.5% loss max—though often, it will end up being breakeven or a slight gain if the stock tries to break through resistance again before falling.

Alternatively, if a trade languishes and goes almost nowhere for 2 weeks, cut it loose. Look for the next entry.

Review:

- Exits determine your profitability.
- Stops protect capital, keep you trading, and help manage emotion.
- Get comfortable with taking profits and training yourself to win.
- Split trades into 3 portions and determine your profit targets.
- Profit targets can be based on percentages that fit your Reward:Risk ratio, or measured targets using technical analysis.
- Typical Profit Targets for Autopilot Trading are at 7-10% (PT1), 17-25% (PT2), and over 30% (PT3) using a trailing stop.
- Taking a portion of your profits early makes it easier to let your winners run.

- If a trade is not behaving as expected from the entry:
  - If you're at least 5% profitable, raise your stop to breakeven or trail at -7.5%.
  - If the trade has gone nowhere, cut it after 2 weeks.

CHAPTER TWELVE

PILLAR 4 - STRATEGIES

When I talk about trading strategy, many people think I'm talking about different tradeable entities: stocks, options, futures, or forex. They might also think I mean the different ways that you can use those tools to create different Reward:Risk profiles, like options strategies, for example. Unfortunately, this is too simplistic.

The challenge is understanding the correlation, or lack thereof, between a trading system and a trading strategy. When we see some of the strategies above, it's easy to get excited about the potential gains and riches available from trading them, so many people think the strategy *is* the system. And the way these things are talked about in the educational space doesn't help. Too often, the newest options or forex "strategy" is presented as all you need to become Scrooge McDuck, swimming in your own pool of cash.

However, attempting to trade a strategy without a comprehensive system is the number one reason traders blow up their accounts and fail in their pursuit of trading success.

The Active Trend Trading system that supports the Auto-Pilot Trading Method was designed to successfully navigate any market condition. With the system as the foundation and the pillars solidly in place, strategies can be layered on top with proven success.

You might find that you prefer certain strategies over others. There are several that match exceptionally well with a swing trading system like ours.

But for simplicity, and to achieve the goal of having a life outside of the market, I strongly encourage traders to start with the simple strategy of buying Stocks and ETFs long (that is, you buy anticipating higher prices). The main reason I recommend a simpler strategy is that there are fewer variables involved.

Charts provide observable VAZs for placing orders to enter and exit. Conditional orders can be easily mastered to give you a "Fire and Forget" approach. While there is some trade or position management, it is simpler than that required by other strategies like options, futures, or forex.

Stocks and ETFs also give you relief from the added pressures of expiration dates (options & futures) or a constantly open market (forex). Not to mention the other complexities of these markets, such as contango and arbitrage. If you've never heard those words, it should show you that you have more to learn before exploring these strategies.

I say master the fundamentals, and you'll always have a way to succeed, even if you choose to try more exotic strategies in the future.

So, what's the best way to engage the strategy of long stock and ETF trades?

Incorporate a complete system around the strategy.

When it comes to being more strategic about that simple strategy, you only need to learn how to manage the position size and the total number of open positions.

Proper Position Sizing

Position sizing is the second element of determining our risk on any given trade (our stop price is the first), and it works to trade any entity type. Stops determine your risk based on the entry price per share. Here, we're figuring out the total dollar amount at risk.

A popular rule of thumb is to calculate your position size based on a potential loss of no more than 1% of total trading capital on any one position. If a trader has $100k in capital, a 1% loss would be $1,000.

To take advantage of multiple opportunities and avoid overburdening ourselves with too many positions, we'll want to balance the per-trade risk with the total number of positions, or portfolio management.

> **NOT SO FAST:** *You might think it's as simple as dividing $1,000 by your potential loss per share. But that might tie up too much capital. If I'm buying right on top of a strong support level and my stop is close enough that my per-share risk is only $1, the easy math suggests that I can buy 1,000 shares. But what if the stock price is over $100? You may not have enough in your account for that position—and you may want to leave capital available for other opportunities.*

Portfolio Management

On an account of $100K or more, a prudent number of open positions is between 4-8. You *might* consider increasing to a max of 10 with a larger account. This minimizes the time and effort spent managing and tracking positions while allowing you to take advantage of multiple opportunities. Depending on how many positions you are comfortable managing, you can easily determine where your catastrophic stop loss should be. Remember that you might have a reason to bring the stop loss closer, but this would be your maximum risk on the position.

On that $100k account, the math would look like this:

- 4 open positions
- $100K/4 = $25K per open position (non-margin).
- $1,000 max loss / $25k invested = .04 or 4% below entry price.

OR maybe:

- 8 open positions
- $100k/8 = $12.5k per position
- $1,000 max loss / $12.5k invested = .08 or 8% below entry price.

NOTE: *Noted the math on some of these examples puts them outside my own maximum catastrophic loss of 5-7% on any trade. These are just examples, and you will have to do the math with your own accounts and risk tolerance.*

More positions allow for more breathing room in the maximum stop loss, which may or may not fit your risk tolerance. Just keep in mind that everyone has their limits on how many positions they can manage at a given time as well. Find the number that works well for you and change if needed.

There's another way to back into a position size. Conventional trading wisdom indicates that initial stop losses should be between 5-10%. We can also calculate proper position sizing by simply dividing the max initial stop loss by the stop loss percentage. So, if my max loss is $1,000 and my stop loss percentage is 10%, my max position size would be $1000/10% = $10K, and the number of positions I could have open would be 10 on a $100K account.

However, I still recommend using technical analysis to find a stop price that is closer to your entry whenever possible.

When you chunk up your portfolio into set position sizes, it makes it easy to determine how many shares to buy. Simply divide your position size by the stock price.

For example:

- $25k position size / $35.22 share price = 709.8 shares (700 shares)
- $12.5k position size / $35.22 share price = 354.9 shares (350 shares)
- $10k position size / $35.22 share price = 283.9 shares (280 shares)

Always round down when determining the final number of shares. It is also advisable to round down to the nearest lot of 5 or 10 because orders in these lots are easier to fill. I prefer lots of 10, but smaller accounts may want to use 5 for a while. By lots, I mean that if the position size/share price equation tells you to buy 709.8 shares as above, round down to 700 (or 705 for lots of 5). Rounding up will increase your risk!

It's also wise to do the math in reverse to ensure that **Number of shares times Loss per share** is within your maximum loss per trade parameters.

When to modify your position sizing

If the market is weak, it is a good idea to reduce position size. I use both technical analysis and Investor's Business Daily's Market Pulse to establish market strength or weakness. If the Market Pulse is "In Confirmed Uptrend," I have a green light to open full positions and go into margin per my rules. If the Market Pulse reports either "Uptrend Under Pressure" or "Market In Correction," I limit stock and ETF purchases to ½ size positions. I still determine my initial stops based on my technical analysis or catastrophic loss as previously described, but I cut the position size in half, which halves my risk.

To be safe, I will also reduce my profit expectations from 10% for PT1 to 5-7% and from 22.5% down to 15-17% for PT2.

If the market proves itself, I may add to that position during a later pullback to the moving averages. That usually means Trigger 4 in the chapter on entries.

> **MARGIN:** *Because margin rules vary between brokers, I'm not going to cover it in this book. Be aware that margin is a double-edged sword. Talk to your broker about how it may change your risk profile and what their rules are.*

Traders who blow up their accounts typically do not follow these trading best practices nor include them in their trading rules. Learning to avoid self-inflicted mistakes will go a long way in helping new traders hang on and make it to being successful, master traders.

Additionally, the above best practices will also ensure a trader is not stressed by holding too many positions. Every great trader, from Bill O'Neil to Mark Minervini, puts a cap on the number of positions they hold and then prunes down until they have 2-5 positions as the winners prove themselves!

Cutting up the Profit Pie

As I said before, learning to take profits is equally important as learning how to enter a trade. There is strategy here, too.

I have found having 3 separate exits planned helps traders accomplish several goals. First, it teaches them how to take profits and protect profits so trades do not turn against them. By scratching that itch to book gains, it allows winners to keep going with the remaining portion.

In the last chapter, the three profit targets below:
- Profit Target 1 (PT1) = 7-10%
- Profit Target 2 (PT2) = 17%-25%
- Profit Target 3 (PT3) = Set at -7.5% trailing stop after PT 1 is hit.
   - Adjust to -12.5% once PT2 is hit.

The actual share split can be 1/3's, but my research has shown that the following portions provide a higher average return even if the 3rd portion hits it's trailing stop.
- At PT1 = Sell 30% of shares
- At PT2 = Sell 50% of shares
- At PT3 = Sell 20% of shares

With one previous example, we purchased 350 shares. Using lots of ten, I might break that into 110 shares (~30% for PT1), 170 shares (~50% for PT2), and 70 shares (20% for PT3).

Designing the Trade

Choosing the earlier example of a $100K account where we want a maximum of 8 positions, let's design a trade.

Our maximum position size is $12.5K, and the entry price we're considering is $35.22.

$12.5k position size / $35.22 share price = 354.9 shares (350 shares)

My maximum stop is $1000/350=$2.85 loss per share. This is just over 8%, and not a favorable R:R ratio. But we were able to find a technical level of support around $34.25. We place our stop $0.10 below that level.

Technical Stop = $34.15 (-3%)

Initial Profit targets: bundle these orders with the stop, as we'll teach later.
PT1 10% = $38.74 (sell 110 shares)
PT2 20% = $42.26 (sell 170 shares)
PT3 30% = $45.78 (sell 70 shares)

When PT1 is hit, I book $387.20 in profits ($3.52 x 110 shares).

I keep my PT2 order in place but change the stop to a trailing stop between 7.5% and 10%, depending on potential support areas. PT3 becomes only the trailing stop.

When PT2 is hit, I book $1,196.80 ($7.04 X 170 shares).

I switch PT3 into a 12.5% trailing stop that triggers whenever it triggers. Worst case, if things turn bad from here, I'll make about 5% on this third portion for a total return of about 13.8%. But sometimes, the market will give a 30% run or more before that significant pullback. Along the way, I may choose to raise that stop if I see good support areas.

I take a few minutes for my daily check after market. If I notice significant resistance, a bearish candlestick pattern, and/or waning momentum (especially with bearish divergence), I may raise my trailing stop to just below the last swing low to protect those profits.

I keep looking for opportunities on the weekend to engage that newly freed-up capital and profit.

Review:

Position sizing caps your maximum loss per trade - recommended at no more than 1% of total capital.

Portfolio management helps you focus by limiting the maximum number of trades you're managing - recommend 4-8 for a $100K account.

Combining the two lets you engage capital and keep efficient management.

Break up your Profit Targets into 3 uneven portions for greater returns.

Let winners run!

CHAPTER THIRTEEN

PILLAR 5 – WHAT TO EXPECT

When I was flying, I had to trust my aircraft. Which meant I had to learn how it performed in different conditions. That led to lots of practice and test flights that measured both the plane's performance and my own.

Similarly, trusting a system requires an understanding of system performance. With a few calculations, you can know how a system has performed in the past (either back testing or live trading) and then project similar performance into the future, assuming that you continue to trade in the same way.

In a perfect world, every trader would trade a system exactly the same way, yielding the same results. But we don't live in a perfect world, so each person's results will be different based on how *they* trade and the choices they make about each piece of the system.

The calculations for measuring a system's performance are the Win:Loss Ratio, Profit: Loss Ratio, Profit Factor, and Expectation. There are also certain expectations that any system requires of a trader. Together, they pull the performance data of both back testing and live trading to establish guidelines for estimating future performance. These metrics define how strong of an edge a particular system has.

Professional traders use them to learn the average profit per dollar invested and then extrapolate into plans and goals for future profitability.

Why does it matter? Because without these calculations, you could be trading your account into the ground by using a system without a keen edge.

As an example, many hyped-up, high-win-rate systems lose money over the long-term, but unsuspecting novice traders fall for the allure of so many wins. Unfortunately, due to inexperience, ignorance, or both, those novices find they keep losing cash even though they have a win rate of 90% or more.

Why?

The answer is in the calculations mentioned above.

A system may have a high Win:Loss Ratio, but if the Profit:Loss ratio, Profit Factor, Expectancy, or Expectations are too low, the system will still be a loser!

We'll have to get into some math to prove it. Let's consider a system that has a respectable Win:Loss Ratio of 65% but the Profit:Loss ratio is only 0.5 per win, or only fifty cents per win to $1 per loss.

The system would have no edge at all.

With 65 of 100 trades the trader earns $0.50 but loses $1.00 on 35 of the trades. So out of 100 trades, the trader would earn $32.5 (65 x $0.50) but lose $35 (35 x $1.00).

No matter how much the trader may brag about winning 65% of his trades, they'll still be a losing trader and wonder why.

In this case, the Profit Factor is too low, and the Expectancy is negative.

We'll explain the details of the different calculations below. This will help you establish the minimum criteria to assess the performance of any trading system you're even thinking about using.

Profit Factor: The Strength of A System's Edge

The Profit Factor must be greater than 1.0 for a system to be a winner. It is calculated as:

$$\frac{(\% \text{ Winning Trades } \times \text{ Avg. Win \$})}{(\% \text{ Losing Trades } \times \text{ Avg. Loss \$})}$$

Using the previous example, (65% wins x $0.50) / (35% losses x $1.00) = ($32.50)/($35.00) = 0.92

If this result is less than 1, the losing factors are greater than the winning factors, which leads to negative overall performance. In other words, this system will lose $$$! And the larger the bottom number is in relation to the top number, the more you will lose.

The inverse is also true. The larger the top number is in relation to the bottom number, the greater your profit.

If you were evaluating the hypothetical system we just measured, it would be back to the drawing board. You could repair the system by figuring out how to increase average gains, reduce average losses, or improve your win-loss ratio.

Expectancy: The Probable Outcome Over Time

The pursuit of a trading system that produces a positive expectancy is critical to trading success. It's even considered by some to be trading's "holy grail."

Expectancy provides an additional measure of performance that will truly reflect the value of a system's edge. It's called expectancy because it reveals what you can expect (what's highly probable) over a large number of trades.

Here's the formula:

Expectancy = (%Wins x Avg. Win $) – (%Losers x Avg. Loss $)

Using the same example above:
(65% wins x $0.50) - (35% losses x $1.00) = 0.325 - 0.35 = -0.025

In this scenario, every trade loses 2.5 cents.

If this equation played out over 100 trades, you would see a -$2.50 loss in total. Your account would very slowly die from papercuts.

However, if you reigned in your losses and let your winners run enough that you could flip the amounts of your gains and losses, you'd be pleased.

(65% wins x $1.00) - (35% losses x $0.50) = 0.65 - 0.175 = 0.475

That's $0.475 per trade, or a $47.50 gain over 100 trades. Not that exciting yet, but let's work with some more realistic numbers, instead of these tiny trades.

(65% x $1,000) - (35% x $500) = $650-$175 = $475

Now, we're looking at the net potential gain of $475 *per trade* on this improved system or $47,500 over 100 trades if performance remains similar.

The new results have a Profit Factor of 3.71 vs the original of 0.92!

Since these calculations are about average results, it's important to remember that the expectancy equation is only accurate over a large number of trades, which can be time-consuming to validate. It's possible to see great results on your first handful of trades and be fooled into thinking your system has a positive expectancy when that's not necessarily the case.

Unfortunately, the time and work involved in validating a system's expectancy discourages most people from even trying. But those who put in the effort to find positive expectancy systems are well on their way to trading success. Plus, they get hundreds or thousands of reps trading their system.

Expectancy can also reveal the Reward:Risk picture of any given trade by entering the actual amount being risked in place of the average loss, and the measured target in place of the average gain.

Other Expectations

How many trades do I need to earn 40% per year?

It Depends! At Least One.

Seriously, it depends on your position sizing and timeframe. First, let's consider someone who trades rarely and uses weekly signals to get into longer-term trades. If a trader applies proper trade and risk management practices and divides capital between 4-8 open positions, then a turn-over could be as low as 20 trades or up to 40 trades for the total portfolio to reach our target. If market conditions reduce the Expectancy of the system, the number of trades could increase. And these estimates may not take into consideration a wider stop loss, for instance, which may be important to catching longer trends. Without testing, I can't speak to that experience of trading longer trends.

In my case, I use daily signals to swing trade on a short to medium-term basis, so I currently trade roughly 100 times per year. That might sound like a lot to some folks. But if we break it down, I'm spending a couple of hours on the weekend and only entering 2-3 trades per week, on average. Some weeks, I don't get any entries, and sometimes, there's a handful.

Also, remember, the system is automated with conditional orders (more on that in the next section), so time commitments are drastically reduced compared to actively watching the market. Once orders are in place, a trader waits for the conditional orders to work and applies necessary trade management to protect both profits and capital.

You're checking on positions and orders for a moment each day. To me, that's worth the returns I see.

What to Expect with the AutoPilot System?

How many trading opportunities are really out there with just one setup?

The targets of opportunity are very plentiful. As an example, the Index ETFs I follow each provide 3-8 setups per year. I follow seven specific ETFs each week. That's 21-56 opportunities per year already, but each follows a different cycle of being ready to trade or not, so the opportunities don't come all at once.

I also track a list of growth stocks, which gives me plenty of opportunities to trade.

My intent is to have up to 7-10 positions open at any one time.

Managing opportunities is sometimes as important as finding them.

So far for 2023, here are my system's numbers (as of 9/17/23):

- Win:Loss Ratio: 49:48
- Profit:Loss Ratio: 1.83:1
- Return: +23%
- Profit Factor: 1.87 (above 1 is profitable)
- Expectancy: $780.36 per trade at average position sizing
- For comparison, the S&P is currently up only 15.91% for the year.

I'll admit, this year my W/L Ratio is off schedule with my yearly goal of 60-65%. However, experience also tells me that the 4th quarter tends to accelerate winning trades, and the W:L Ratio will finish the year at or above the yearly goal and boost my returns closer to my annual target. On the upside, these numbers reveal that you can be very profitable even with a 50/50 win ratio, as long as your Reward:Risk is properly managed.

What to Expect in Yourself?

In trading there are two connected yet separate psychologies traders must adapt to or forever be mediocre or even losing traders! Market Psychology and Personal Trading Psychology.

Market Psychology encompasses billions of combined behaviors of all the market participants. What is remarkable is how these combined behaviors are revealed on stock or index price charts. The charts show significant reference points where the aggregate of trader beliefs and expectations are met. Support and Resistance are two of the most obvious of those points.

Learning to become a neutral observer and understand the meaning of these significant reference points will greatly help traders master their own psychological challenges when it comes to trading. A great book that digs deeply into Market Psychology is *The Disciplined Trader* by Mark Douglas & Dr. Paula Webb. This book also has a workbook called *Becoming "The Disciplined Trader"* that can help you implement his strategies.

A trader's personal trading psychology determines how a trader perceives Market Psychology. Personal trading psychology connects our beliefs (both true and false) about money, trading, charts, trading systems, and much more. Included in the psychological mix is mindset, self-perception, and self-belief! Some refer to a trader's personal psychology as psychological capital. The higher the psychological capital, the better a trader can weather the ebbs and flows of their system and their own performance in the market.

To dig deeper into personal psychology, I suggest reading *The Trading Mindwheel* by Michael Lamothe or, more broadly, *Mindset Secrets for Winning* by Mark Minervini. You can find my full reading list at AutoPilotTraders.com/ReadingList.

We can modify our psychological habits and routines to form a winning mindset and winning routine. I have found that my trading system is impacted by my psychology in both directions. When my system or routine is poor, it negatively impacts my emotional resilience while trading. An unrealistic attitude can also sway how I engage my trading system. Ultimately, you have to manage the external routine and the internal mindset.

I believe the best way to learn and manage trading emotions is to trade a mechanical trading system. It reduces impulsive decisions by putting clear boundaries around approved trades. When you set yourself up for making better decisions, it's easier to control the self-talk. Either you traded the rules, or you didn't. The outcome then breaks down according to your system's expectancy.

Additionally, I perform all analysis and mechanical trade setups during non-market hours and use automation to remove potential emotional traps. Learning how to set up trades with automated conditional orders during non-market hours will greatly reduce most negative aspects of faulty trading psychology and habits.

$$|_{+}\phi|^{\phi}_{\parallel}$$

A great example of how this approach can help eliminate poor trading habits is for the trader who refuses to use stop losses. Failure to place mechanical stop losses reflects a trader with ego issues. They believe that when a price action hits a stop level, they will have the wherewithal to close the position. Unfortunately, this is typically not the case. The trader will hang onto the position and let the loss grow and turn into a painful experience. This is a clear case of operator error! If the trader recognizes that this is an issue and the pain of losing capital becomes great enough, they will learn how to place conditional orders that will close the position at a preset stop loss! Once a trader learns these valuable lessons and takes wise action, they are on their way to becoming a wise, disciplined and profitable trader.

It surprises many new traders, but trading makes demands on our physical, mental, emotional, and even spiritual resources. You aren't just investing your money, because your beliefs and feelings about money go along with it. If you're tired or in poor health, it can affect your trading. If you're stressed or worried, it can affect your trading. So, consider more than just the money when you consider planning your trading and wealth strategy.

If you're in a season with almost zero free time, consider limiting your trading to just one or two entities for the time being. If you're experiencing extra stress or health issues, you might trade smaller positions to limit the cost of mistakes or stress-influenced decisions. Or you might take a temporary break from trading if you're facing a major crisis. Make sure you're taking care of your whole self, or the money won't do much good.

Using These Tools for Wealth Planning Through "Strategic Accelerated Compounding"

Compounding used to be a common topic when discussing wealth-building. Now, we primarily talk about returns and don't hear much about the amazing power of compounding and time. That's a shame because without understanding this concept, it's easy to make decisions that can sabotage your wealth plans.

Most people think of compounding as only the habit of reinvesting returns to increase your total outcome. But when you grasp the interplay between returns and time (including reinvesting gains), you can be strategic about compounding. With the tools mentioned above, you can create a wealth plan that incorporates hard data to get you to the desired outcome before you start. It's like creating your very own wealth map using real data and math to plot your course. Then you simply have to follow through.

I call this method of data-driven planning "Strategic Accelerated Compounding." It's a dynamic strategy that capitalizes on the remarkable potential of compound interest while making shrewd investment decisions.

Rather than focusing on one big number as your goal for wealth accumulation, Strategic Accelerated Compounding breaks that big goal down into smaller goals and milestones along the way. For it to be accelerated, it requires higher than average returns, like those offered by the AutoPilot Trading Method.

If you ask the average person how much a 40% annual return would be if broken down into quarters, they will assume you earned 10% per quarter, or 3.33% per month. But if you reinvest your returns to engage compounding, you only need 8.78% per quarter or 2.85% per month to *surpass* a 40% annual return.

Does 2.85% per month sound like a lot? I hope not.

Knowing this information can help you plan and strategize for the mile markers along the path to your retirement goal.

As you're trading, it also allows you to track your progress easily! If I know I'm shooting for 8.75% per quarter, it only takes a few moments to check my progress if I'm keeping up-to-date records. After several years (or with enough backward research), you'll notice seasonal patterns in your results that can help you further refine your projections and tracking metrics.

Obviously, this won't work with a buy and hold method that relies on chance for when you get into and out of each investment. You need a system that manages risk, engages precise timing of entries and exits, and allows for monitoring and adjustments like the AutoPilot Trading Method. It also helps to find entities that move at least the amount you want to attain every quarter.

To share a brief example, the Proshares leveraged ETF for the Nasdaq 100 (TQQQ) has been known for consistent quarterly returns of at least 20% since 2011. If you were able to capture that move, it would compound annually at over 100 percent. Just getting half of that move gets you 46.41%, which well exceeds our annual goal.

The power of compounding rests in the rate of return, and the frequency with which it compounds. Our goal is to increase both so that our money is constantly growing instead of growing and then shrinking, like the rest of the market.

Just as a thought exercise, if you were able to perfectly trade the TQQQ and get that 20% per quarter, the results would be astonishing. It would take a $1,000 investment and turn it into approximately $1,469,771.57 in just 10 years.

This astounding growth is a testament to the potential rewards of compounding, especially when coupled with a well-executed strategy like the AutoPilot Method.

By diligently adhering to the rules of the system, you can harness the true power of compounding and chart your own course. With discipline and patience, your wealth may flourish at an accelerated pace, ultimately propelling you closer to your financial aspirations.

Review:

Math can tell us how a system will perform over time.

- Profit Factor – Whether a system *can* be profitable. This equation tells you the strength of a system's edge.
- Expectancy – The average gain or loss per trade based on past performance over a period of time.
- Expectations – The mindset, beliefs, attitudes, and habits that will affect your personal performance when trading your system. Includes understanding the reality of what your system is capable of under similar performance and what you are able to handle at any given time.
- Strategic Compounding – Breaking down your annual goal into quarterly chunks reveals that you need a lower return the more frequently you lock in gains and reinvest them. This can help you plan your future and have markers to measure your ongoing progress.

HOW TO GET STARTED WITH AUTOPILOT TRADING NOW

HOW TO GET STARTED WITH AUTOPILOT TRADING NOW

CHAPTER FOURTEEN

TOOLS YOU NEED TO GET STARTED

I started this book by telling you that it had three sections with three main ideas. First, that you can grow your wealth easier and faster with a clear and simple trading system. Second, that mastering a system with a simple trade set up gives you more than enough opportunity to grow faster than the market over the long-term.

We are finally in the third section, where the main idea is to show you how to take advantage of those first two ideas by incorporating the AutoPilot Trading Method into your trading life. This is the execution stage, where we will share our favorite tools and habits to get the AutoPilot Trading Method working for you.

You don't need much to start trading. Really, you only need to minimally fund a trading account and figure out how to hit the buy button. That's why "easy" trading platforms like Robin Hood are so popular. But I hope you see—that's the road to losses.

The road to trading in a way that gives you a solid chance of growing your wealth—like we've been teaching you—requires a few extra tools to make the difference.

Here they are:

A funded account: Of course, you need money to trade. A minimally funded account looks different depending on the brokerage you choose. If you remember back to the Roadmap chapter, our starting assumption was $18,000. I'll repeat that this is a healthy amount to start with if you have solid money management principles and habits in place.

If you start with more, it will obviously be a faster road, though it won't necessarily make it easier to master the system. However, there are account size thresholds that lead to fewer restrictions. Check with your broker about those.

A trading and charting platform: Your brokerage will have some research and charting capabilities through its website. There are also plenty of more advanced software programs for detailed technical charts. My favorite mix for functionality and customization is ThinkorSwim, now owned by Schwab. Use what works for you, but this is the platform that I use for all of my example charts and videos.

A good source for solid growth stocks: This can be a list you purchase, or it can come from your own research. Earlier, I told you about my preferred source for those lists and how I sort them for my own purposes. Our Autopilot Trading Service narrows that list even more and includes details about how I plan to engage a handful of potential trades each week. Whatever source you use, remember to keep your list manageable.

A disciplined routine: This is probably the most important tool in your arsenal. I explored plenty of reasons why you need it in part one of this book, so for now, I'll just say, "Discipline is the vehicle to get you to your goals."

- ◆ Your routine should help you work through each of the first 5 pillars when you're making trading decisions.
- ◆ Does this trade follow the system rules for the first 5 Pillars: what to trade, when to enter, when to exit, proper strategy, and expectation? Are you consistently using tools like the Precision Entry Points Routine when you do your trade prep?
- ◆ The disciplined side of this comes in how consistently you carry out your routine. Decide when and where you will do your research, order entry, and tracking each week. Put it in your calendar or as a reminder on your phone. Then, keep that appointment.

Mindset: I mentioned this earlier as well, so for now, I'll just reiterate that you need to understand yourself and the market if you want to come out as a winner in this game.

Recordkeeping: Like many other parts of the system, record-keeping isn't sexy. But it's the only way to know whether you're getting closer to being a successful trader or if you just got lucky (or unlucky). Without a record of what you did, you'll never know how you can improve or even how disciplined you have been.

The remainder of this third section of the book will go into more detail on the pieces of this list that will help you get started.

Take Action!

Write out your own notes and plan for each item below:
- • Funded Account

- Trading/Charting Platform
- Source of Growth Stocks/ETFs
- Research Routine - Including stock parameters and trading rules.
- Are you in a healthy, neutral mindset that allows you to see the setup and follow the system rules? Are you willing to trust the system and not make system-level changes over any single trade?
- How will you keep yourself disciplined to follow your plan and keep the right mindset?

CHAPTER FIFTEEN

TRAINING, TESTING, AND SIMULATION

Training is essential. It incorporates discipline, mindset, and other skills that will help you on your path. You're gaining some training by reading this book. Reading it twice would profit you more. Reading it and implementing the steps involved would profit you most.

Study the system until it makes sense to you. Test and simulate with past market data. Then, take your knowledge out into the real market to see if you can apply it on live charts (but not necessarily risking real money yet).

Here's what that looks like:

First, dedicate some time in your routine to studying charts and finding the PEP setup pattern. Train your brain to recognize it until you can pick it out quickly on any chart. Do the same with the candlestick patterns in the appendix. Get to recognize the characteristics until you can spot these things like second nature.

The next step is testing. Spotting candlestick patterns and setups in isolation is a start. But they don't do you much good unless you bring in the other portions of the system. Back testing is a great way to continue practicing, but more importantly, it helps prove the concept to you and increases confidence in yourself *and* the system.

Back testing is the process of pulling up old charts and scrolling back in time to a random spot, then rolling forward at a comfortable pace where you can recognize signals and pretend to trade them. When you record the results of that simulated trade (honestly) and run through many of those simulations, you begin to get a sense for how well the system works and how well you're able to implement it at your current skill level. It also shows you some of the real-life challenges and nuances of recognizing signals and trading according to the system.

Do a few trades at a time instead of running through multiple years on a chart. You'll avoid burnout and simulate the natural breaks we take from the market.

Back testing should be done with the intent of proving the viability of the system with your current skill set. In my experience, back testing leads to elevated returns because of the lack of emotions involved and sometimes the ability to over-optimize the test. It's still a great method to get reps and boost your confidence.

ThinkorSwim has a new tool that enhances the realism of back testing. Their On-Demand feature lets you go back to old charts and play them forward like video while making simulated trades within their platform.

Unlike traditional back testing, in which you step forward one candlestick at a time, this one shows the rising and falling of each candlestick as it formed. Their historic data gets played back in a sped-up time frame, so you can get a lot of reps of practice in a realistic setting.

The downside is that it's not as fast as traditional back testing, but the upsides far outweigh this. You can practice placing real trades on the platform since the On-Demand back testing feature works exactly like the live trading function. This builds the habit of placing trades. You can also become accustomed to letting trades play out according to your predetermined plan (instead of second-guessing every few candles). This further trains your brain and body to trust the system regardless of what the market does. It can reduce the positive bias in old back testing methods and get a more realistic view of your potential results.

Just be certain that you test a significant amount of data so that you have a decent sample size. Don't extrapolate potential based on a handful of trades, because every trading system is based on a large number of trades over time. I recommend starting with 3-5 trades per practice session, as often as you have time available.

Think of it like your wealth gym.

The more reps, the better you get!

Check out the video on using this feature, along with the other videos and tutorials on the book's bonus resources webpage <u>AutoPilotTraders.com/Print-Resources</u>. It's probably getting old, but use the coupon code PRINT100 and it's free.

Simulation is the final tool to continue developing discipline and mindset. The on-demand feature is as close as we can get to a real-time simulation in which we can increase our personal repetitions of the steps of making trading decisions in a compressed timeframe. However, there are also paper trading platforms that let you make those decisions in current market conditions.

Paper trading is when a platform lets you place simulated trades in the current market using pretend account money. It's like Monopoly for the stock market. ThinkorSwim has a paper trading side that you can experiment with as well. This helps build the patience muscle even more than the on-demand simulator.

Before risking real money, I highly recommend using both back testing and forward testing by paper trading. You'll learn so much that will serve you as long as you trade.

How much you decide to paper trade and for how long is up to you. But I have said for years that <u>a trader needs to experience at least one hundred trades with a system in order to gain proficiency with it</u>. That gets you to proficiency—not mastery!

Forward testing through paper trading is the best way to overcome any positive biases that existed in your back testing, and it begins to introduce some of the emotions inherent in the live market. Without real money at risk, your emotions won't be engaged entirely, but you are more likely to act according to your natural tendencies and experience some emotions in paper trading versus back testing.

These simulations are exactly like what I engaged in as a naval pilot. Airline pilots do the same; they have to qualify in simulated emergencies in order to keep flying. And trust me, they experience emotions in their simulators!

If you don't want to crash and burn with your real account, put it through the simulator. If you want to evaluate your performance from the past year and see if you could've done better, put it through the back testing simulators.

When you begin adding real risk to your practice, consider starting with just a few shares at a time to add more confirmation to your confidence in the system.

If you start out making practice a part of your routine, you'll be setting yourself up for a lifetime of success instead of a flash in the pan before blowing up an account.

Take Action!

- ◆ Review the AutoPilot Trading rules. Refer to the relevant chapters in this book, as needed, or use the rules on 1-page here on the resources page linked below.
- ◆ Once you feel comfortable picking out the setup from the PEP Routine, set some goals for training.
  - ○ How many trades will you back test?
  - ○ How many trades will you paper trade?
  - ○ When and how will you introduce risk?
- ◆ Download my Trader Tools for tracking practice and real trades. Also on the resources page at <u>AutoPilot-Traders.com/Print-Resources</u>. Once more, the coupon code is PRINT100.

CHAPTER SIXTEEN

A REAL MONEY ROUTINE

Trading routines have one aim: Be Ready to Trade!

MINDSET FIRST: *"Are you ready to give yourself money?" Mark Minervini checks his readiness by asking himself this question at the beginning of each trading day.*

Just as professional athletes use routines for peak performance, a good routine can keep you trading efficiently and effectively.

An efficient routine answers 3 primary questions:
- What are overall market conditions?
- Are any of the stocks on your list near a trigger, or has one fired?
- What must you do to be ready to trade those potential triggers?

To be efficient, consider limiting the number of stocks on your watchlist—and stop looking when you find a handful of potential opportunities.

Then, prepare a routine of how you'll evaluate those opportunities in an efficient way.

Below are my primary routine habits:

Research
What time will you research and what time will you trade? How long will you schedule research?

Review
Will you review the market and your watchlist after hours or pre-open?

Setups
Check potential setups. Have any circumstances changed?

Updates
Any upcoming news or announcements to keep in mind?

Alerts/Orders
Check or place alerts on potential setups (if you have the ability and self-control to check things intra-day)

Place orders on positively identified setups, or check existing orders.

Adjust stops and profit targets if orders have filled or conditions have changed.

Journal & Log
Journal your setups or filled trade details, and log closed trades.

Other

Any other personal routines or details that will help you with trading, like reading, nutrition, exercise, trading simulation, or even prayer.

My preference is to do all my research and preparation after hours, automating the actual trade execution with conditional orders to buy and sell. That's how I remove impulsive decisions and give myself the room to live LIFE!

Write out a trade routine that works for your lifestyle on the first page of your journal, or on a sheet of paper. Don't let it hide on your computer, but have it available for regular reference, along with your rules.

Put your routine in your schedule, try it out, and adjust as necessary.

Trading Goals

Trading goals encompass more than just returns. Almost more important are trading goals that aim at your own progress as a trader. Consider goals that target your consistency, education, and habits. After all, you can't control the markets; you can only control your own actions.

Consider appropriate rewards if you meet the action goals you set.

Better yet, let the process of consistent action *be* the reward. There is compelling scientific research that learning to enjoy the process is the fastest route to achievement and contentment.

To help you accomplish the goals you set, take on only a handful of big things for the year, and chunk them down into smaller pieces for each quarter or month.

Make sure each goal has a compelling, emotional reason for you to reach it, or it's unlikely you'll put in the effort.

Recordkeeping:

Smart traders keep good records. Yes, your broker will send you the annual report with all of your trades in it for tax purposes. But if you rely on that report for your records, your trading performance will suffer.

Recordkeeping begins with journaling.

A trade journal is an important tool to help you improve. Keep it simple with just enough information to help you understand *what* you were trading and *why*. You can see a sample of my trade journal pages in the on the resources webpage AutoPilotTraders.com/Print-Resources, if you are planning to write them out yourself. If you want one that's fill-in-the-blank, we have those available for sale on Amazon at https://amzn.to/3CfjtFW (sponsored link).

I find that it's easiest to keep the trade journal consistent if I run it through the first five pillars as I write. What am I trading? Where will I enter and why? Where will I exit (profit or loss) and why? What is my trading strategy, including number of shares, amount at risk, potential profit, etc.? What is my expectation: how confident am I in this trade's potential? Why? Is it because of market activity, convergence of clues, etc.?

With practice, you can write down the answers to these questions in just a couple of minutes and have enough information to be able to look at your journal and a chart several years from now and reconstruct your trade. More importantly, you'll understand your thought process and be able to determine if you made any mistakes in execution. Maybe you got scared because of some news and bailed early, not following your plan. Maybe you got greedy and bailed late after the trend had exhausted itself. Write that stuff in the notes. It will help you do better next time.

The journal helps you know if you did the one thing you can control—manage your own actions.

I also do an annual review of my journal to fairly judge my trading activity. Put that in your calendar while you plan.

The second half of recordkeeping is recording actual trades in a trading log. Your <u>journal</u> might include trades that you never entered because the market didn't hit your trigger. But your <u>trading log</u> will include only those trades that triggered, those where your order filled.

Good recordkeeping will also be a benefit come tax time. Keep up with this habit regularly, and your accountant will thank you (especially if you do your own taxes!)

Set aside the time in your schedule to do both journaling and recordkeeping so that it doesn't get away from you and become a massive chore. I work the system on my weekend prep method. So, I do both my research and recordkeeping at times that are convenient for me.

Review can be done according to your preferred timeline. I would include a look at your trade log records first to see if there are any major outliers in your results. It will also show you if you are close to hitting your targets or if you might need to make some tweaks. If you notice any outliers, go to your journal to evaluate those trades. Make an honest assessment of whether you followed the rules of your system.

<u>Following the rules means a successful trade, even if it lost.</u>

<u>Breaking your rules means an unsuccessful trade, even if it won.</u>

If you need to make any adjustments to your routine or, more rarely, your rules. Review will highlight ideas for those improvements. Run changes by a trusted mentor or colleague, then test them as we discussed in the chapter on back testing and paper trading.

In the early stages, you might review more frequently, even every week. This will help you to reinforce your trading routine and your trading plan. With more experience, you may do a review once a month or once per quarter. In addition, I always do the previously mentioned annual review to evaluate my performance over the long-term and prepare me for tax season.

If I need to make adjustments, I almost always see it during this annual review because I have more data. Putting these things in your routine helps them become a regular occurrence rather than being a major chore. If you are successfully following your rules and your trading plan, your review will also give you the positive reinforcement and feedback to continue. And a growing account should, as well.

Continuing education

Schedule some time to read or watch educational videos to continue learning the nuances of the market. I would not include watching financial TV or commentators in this as the daily market battle is not so much education as simple reporting and is soaked in opinion and noise. That will only add confusion. By education, we mean studying excellent traders and their methods, studying technical charting, or continuing back testing and simulations.

If you believe in the power of the AutoPilot system, I would caution you on venturing into investing content that is extremely different in method. It's easy to begin the journey and take a detour before you've attained mastery. Whenever possible, it's more helpful to stay the course of your current education than jump to something new.

If you would like further help from us in learning the system or getting a handle on your routine, visit AutoPilotTraders.com/membership. Use coupon code FREEDOM10 to get a discount for buying the book.

Take Action!

Write out a draft routine with all the relevant points:

Research
What time will you research and what time will you trade? How long will you schedule research?

Review
Will you review the market and your watchlist after hours or pre-open?

Setups
Check potential setups. Have any circumstances changed?

Updates
Any upcoming news or announcements to keep in mind?

Alerts/Orders
Check or place alerts on potential setups (if you have the ability and self-control to check things intra-day)

Place orders on positively identified setups, or check existing orders.

Adjust stops and profit targets if orders have filled or conditions have changed.

Journal & Log

Journal your setups, filled trade details, and log closed trades.

Other

Any other personal routines or details that will help you with trading.

Gather any materials or tools you will use to keep journals and logs.

Decide on what books or other educational content you will consume this year that will help you master this style of trading.

CHAPTER SEVENTEEN

AUTOMATING THE TRADE: THE MECHANICS OF FREEDOM

In this last technical section, we'll cover the linchpin that makes it possible for me to claim it's easy to trade at a professional level even if you're strapped for time: Automating the trade.

Even if you choose to pursue a different system, this particular piece of our method will work for you and improve your results.

While plenty of trainers encourage you to automate parts of your trade, like setting a stop automatically, I've spent the last few years refining the technique to a degree that I call it AutoPilot Trading.

As you'll see, I can say that because I'm able to set up my entry trigger, protective stop, and profit targets all in one order block. If the market decides to hit my entry and my first target in one day, I don't have to do anything extra to lock in profit (or protect myself from losses).

This is what gives me more time freedom, while the results of the system give me more financial freedom.

Learning to place automated orders also reinforces the routine required to follow the trading rules of the system.

The process of recognizing the PEP setup, identifying VAZs, and sizing the position provides the framework for consistency! Achieving consistency leads to efficient use of time. Many traders waste a lot of time trying to find great stocks or ETFs to trade every weekend. They expend so much energy that often they don't finish the job and place their orders. (I know I struggled with that in the past.) Having an efficient system can provide the step ladder to get over this planning weakness.

With a well-curated list like we discussed in Pillar 1, the AutoPilot Trading process takes most traders less than 2 hours per week for analysis and order entry. Let's get into the mechanics so you can enjoy trading with more time freedom.

Take a look at any trading platform and one finds there are many Order Types. If you're not familiar with order types, I recommend checking out a general information source like Investopedia.com so we can keep this discussion brief.

I prefer using **limit** or **stop** orders to enter trades.

A **limit order** tells your broker to fill the order at a specific price (say $35.70) or better. Better is relative. If you're buying, the order will fill at your price or less; if you're selling, the order will fill at your price or more.

Stop orders work when the price has crossed your chosen threshold. Typically, those are sell orders. If you want to protect profits, you might set your stop at $32.15. If the price goes below that, your sell order will fill. In some cases, you might also use a stop order to buy, in which case, the order would fill if the price went above your price ($35.70 in the above example).

Trailing stops are a dynamic option that can help you protect profits as the price moves in your favor. We mentioned them in Pillar 3. In this case, your order moves your stop up as the price moves up. You can often choose to move it up by either a percentage of the current price or a specific dollar amount, based on your broker.

In addition to using these two order types frequently, I also do everything I can to hide my intention from the Market Makers.

Hiding the specifics about my orders from the Market Maker is a throwback to when I first started trading. The Market Makers could see the price levels of where traders were stacking both entry and stop loss orders. Then they would play games like trying to get traders to chase entry prices by keeping bid-ask spreads slightly above desired entries. On the stop loss side, the Market Maker would "Run the Stops," pushing price action down until the stops were hit and then immediately taking prices back up. With the development of modern trading platforms like ThinkorSwim, many brokers hold orders until the price is actually hit, and the Market Maker is never sure of where traders are attempting to take actions of either entering or exiting a position. All they have is information about support and resistance from the charts—the same picture everyone else has—at least in theory.

Check out the specific order types offered by your broker. Some brokers are more flexible than others when it comes to building trade orders. I prefer ThinkorSwim because they provide top-notch flexibility in placing orders.

To increase the flexibility of my orders, I use another method called Conditional Orders—also referred to as

Contingency Orders by some traders and brokers. Conditional Orders allow me to further control when my orders are executed by inserting specific market conditions that I choose. I can trigger the order based on price action or time parameters.

These provide a simple if-then condition for the trading platform to confirm before making my order live. For example, IF the price is below $48.20, THEN submit my stop loss at $48.05.

With some platforms, you can also stack conditions. For example, IF the price is between $26.75-$27.10 (my VAZ), AND the time is after 3PM Eastern (the last hour of the day), THEN submit my buy limit order for $27.20.

This example would automatically purchase the stock only if the price was in your VAZ during the final hour and then started bouncing off that support zone. While you might not get that granular, I hope you can see how powerful this tool is for executing orders exactly how and when *you* choose!

Below, I'll share the specific tricks I use that allow me to set up my entire trade on AutoPilot _before_ I buy, and usually before the market is even open.

Here's a more detailed example of an Entry Conditional Order and the decision process.

Analog Devices (ADI) passes the required fundamental checks and shows tradable technical patterns. A review of the stock chart below shows it bouncing off support at the 200-day moving average (slow-moving dotted line), about $97.

After bouncing around this level for several days, with positive divergence building on the TSI, I know we're in a Value Action Zone. While I wait for a candle reversal pattern to confirm, the support holds, and TSI continues as divergent.

Finally, we get a close above the 8-day Moving average (quick-moving solid line). This is trigger 3, but it happens on a large bullish candle, so I use one of my special conditions to set my trade trap near the middle of the large candle or the moving average. That puts my conditional order to buy shares around $99.24, which I enter as a variation on a limit order (my price or better). This order will not trigger unless price action drops to $99.24 or less.

Here's my variation. If I want an added level of privacy from the market makers, I can make the order conditional upon the stock crossing a certain threshold before my order is submitted. That tells the computer at the broker, "If this stock drops below X, then submit my order." The condition, X, could be just above, or exactly at my limit order since the signals are all instantaneous.

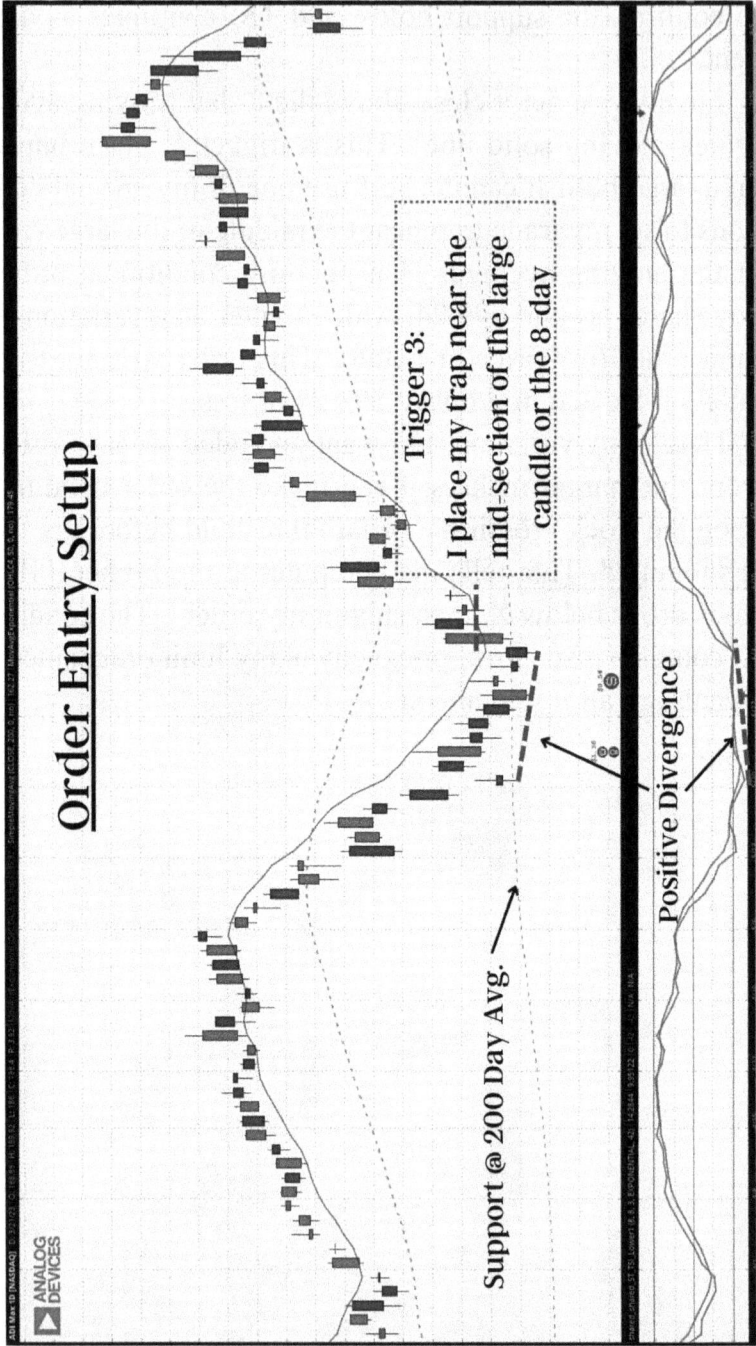

Order Entry Setup.

Trigger 3:
I place my trap near the mid-section of the large candle or the 8-day

Support @ 200 Day Avg.

Positive Divergence

While Market Makers no longer have access to orders placed with certain brokers, they still have a pretty good idea of where buyers and sellers are lining up simply because they understand the habits of traders when it comes to placing orders for entry and exit.

On top of the condition, I include a time requirement. How long would a pullback potentially take to bring price action to $99.24 from the big day's closing price of $100.97? With this type of example, it's typically only a few days.

I'll make the order GTC (Good Till Canceled). This means the order will stay in place until I cancel it. Some brokers have an internal clock that will cancel the order after a set period of days. Check with your broker to see what limits they have. As part of my routine with ThinkorSwim, when I set a GTC Order on the entry, I also set a specific Cancel Date. Typically, I leave orders in place for a week so my entry order will self-destruct on Friday AMC (After Market Close).

The benefit of using this type of entry is that it allows me to plan the trade during the unemotional, non-market hours. I do not have to check this stock until the order is either filled or canceled. I'll simply get a notification that one of those two things happened—and I don't particularly care either way.

What if I want to keep a little closer eye on this pick before my order triggers? To get an early warning of when the price is moving towards my desired entry price, I'll place an alert at a price approaching the entry price. I use $0.10 – $1.00 as a cushion above the desired entry price for this alert. When the alert is triggered, I receive an email or text message notifying me that prices are close to the entry price. If I have the flexibility, I can check the chart at that point to see if there is any slight adjustment I should make to the entry order, perhaps because it's finding support on the 30-minute chart a little higher than my price. But that's only if I have the flexibility to look while the market's open and discipline to follow my rules.

Bundling The Whole Trade For "Fire and Forget"

When I'm designing a trade, I never just place a buy order without also placing my exit orders. Almost all brokers allow me to set up a follow-on exit order if the original buy order is filled. Again, ThinkorSwim is superbly flexible and allows me to automate both potential exit scenarios.

In the example of buying my ADI at $99.24, if this order is filled, it will then instruct my broker to exit where I want. At a minimum, I want a stop loss to be placed if my purchase order fills. Even better, with the right platform, I can place two or three GTC orders with no expiration. These will exit at my pre-defined profit target OR at my stop loss.

A common question is, "What happens if the stock is so volatile that it hits both the stop and the target in the same day?"

Easy: These exit orders are set up so that if one of them fills, the other is automatically canceled. This parameter is called One Cancels Other (OCO).

With ThinkorSwim, I can set this exit order up to sell all the shares or just a part of the shares. This way, I can have the filled entry order engage several potential exit orders according to my rules. Remember how I like to break my exit orders into 3 parts? We can automate that before we ever get into the trade!

My preference is to break the position unequally. First, **at PT1, I sell 30% of the shares, then 50% of the shares at**

PT2, and the final 20% at PT3. On the other side of each of these portions is an initial stop loss.

An example of this setup is below:

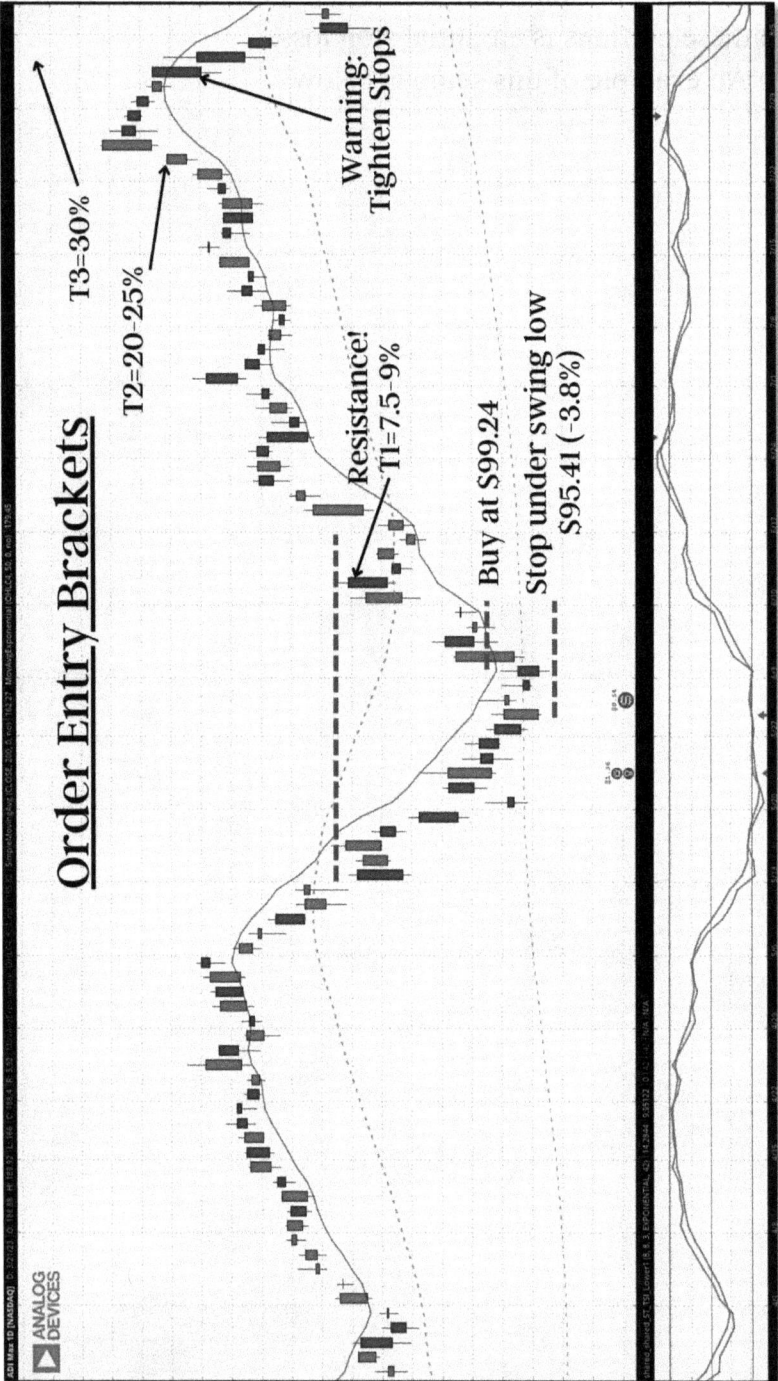

Order Entry Brackets

T3=30%

T2=20-25%

Warning:
Tighten Stops

Resistance!
T1=7.5-9%

Buy at $99.24

Stop under swing low
$95.41 (-3.8%)

"Fire and Forget" Order Entry

Most people are used to using a Market or Limit Order. Market means you're buying at the going price. Limit means you set your maximum buy price, and if the price meets that number or less, your order will fill. I prefer to place a condition on my market order that mimics a limit order, hiding my intentions from the market makers and allowing me to target shoot for the price I want.

As mentioned before, I bundle the entry and all three exits, so this is fire and forget. To do that, I place a specific type of order that ThinkorSwim allows called 1st Triggers 3 OCO. That means that the first order (the buy) initiates 3 separate pairs of sell orders that are "One Cancels Other." In each pair, the order that triggers first will fill and cancel the other one. That's how I can have a stop and a profit target working at the same time.

Note: These orders are typically placed during the weekend. That's why they cancel out the following Friday if the buy order is not filled.

In this case, my order would look like this.

1st Triggers 3 OCO
- Buy to Open 100 Shares ADI.
- This is a market order that is Good Till Canceled (GTC).
- I add a further condition that the order will not be sent unless ADI is <= $99.24.
- I also place a condition to automatically cancel this order if not filled by Friday After Market Close (AMC).

- This is just the opening order. This order type is not complete until I have my 3 exit OCO pairs.

IF ADI drops down to $99.24 or less, my platform will send the market order, and my purchase will fill.

IF the entry order fills, it will create the following 3 unique OCO order pairs to exit, all Good Till Canceled.

Exit Order Pair 1:

The first order in each pair covers my initial stop and that specific portion's profit target. In ThinkorSwim, I can simply right-click on my entry order and create an opposite order to start the exits.

Exit order 1A: This order is OCO, so whichever fills first cancels the other.
- Sell 30 shares ADI (30% of position).
- Market order, GTC.
- Remove the automatic cancelation time from the entry order.
- Create 2 conditions for the order to be submitted.
  - ADI is >= $108.50 (my PT1, about 9% gain).
  - ADI is <= $95.41(my stop of -3.8%).
  - (Note this is a mechanical 2.36:1 Profit:Loss Ratio).

Exit order 1B: This order is in the OCO pair with the one above, so whichever fills first cancels the other. In ThinkorSwim I duplicate the previous order and adjust as so:
- Change from Market order to Trail Stop order.
  - Set trailing stop to a percentage of the Mark price at -7.5%.
- Remove the stop loss condition to sell <= $95.41.

- Adjust the condition to trigger 0.5% lower than PT1 when ADI is >=$107.67 (8.5% instead of 9%).

How does this work? If ADI hits my stop, I will sell at a loss for $95.41. But if ADI reaches my first target at $108.50, then order 1A will sell that portion of shares and cancel order 1B. If the price gets close to my target but weakens after touching $107.67 but before reaching PT1, then order 1B will initiate a trailing stop that should get me out with a slight gain.

Exit Order Pair 2:

Exit Order 2A: In ThinkorSwim, I duplicate both orders from exit order 1 and modify as follows:
- Sell 50 shares ADI (50% of position).
- Modify Condition One to reflect PT2.
  - ADI is >= $119.08 (my PT2 at +20%).
  - Leave the stop condition in place.

Exit order 2B: This order is in the OCO pair with the one above, so whichever fills first cancels the other. Remember, we duplicated both orders from OCO #1, so this should look like order 1B.
- Adjust the number of shares.
- No further modifications.

How does this work? If ADI hits my stop, I will sell at a loss for $95.41. But at $107.67, this order will place a trailing stop of -7.5% on my second chunk. The 50% portion is now protected, guaranteed profit, and will continue to increase as the price goes higher. If ADI reaches PT2 at $119.08, it will sell and cancel the trailing stop. If the price rallies higher but fails to reach my target, I will sell at 7.5% below the highest price, protecting my profits.

Exit Order Pair 3:

Exit Order 3A: In ThinkorSwim, I duplicate both orders from exit order 2 and modify as follows:
- Sell 20 shares ADI (remaining 20% of position).
- Remove Condition 1: the profit Target.
  - ~~ADI is >= $119.08 (my PT2 at +20%)~~
  - Leave the stop condition in place.

Exit order 3B: This order is in the OCO pair with the one above, so whichever fills first cancels the other. Remember, we duplicated both orders from OCO #2, so this should look like order 2B.
- Adjust the number of shares.
- No further modifications.

How does this work? If ADI hits my stop, I will sell at a loss for $95.41. But at $107.67, this order will place a trailing stop of -7.5% on my third chunk. As with OCO pair 2, the 20% portion is now protected, guaranteed profit, and will continue to increase as the price goes higher. Ideally, I hope that this portion will run 30% or more before the trailing stop gets hit.

After PT2 is hit, I prefer to give this last leg some room to run, so I will usually widen the trailing stop to -12.5% or just below a swing low if I see good support. If you want to get even more strategic, you could also enter this one as an OCO, with one side being the trailing stop and the other being a market order with the condition to trigger just below the support zone of a swing low. However, wait until you hit PT2 to make this change.

I know that looks like a lot to set up. With practice, it does get easier. But here's what frontloading all my orders does for me.

When my entry order fills, I get a notification, but I don't have to DO anything. If some bad news hits the market and everything falls, my whole position is protected. If this stock decides to go on a tear that day and hit my first two profit targets, I'm thrilled. And I know I have the chance for bigger gains with the last portion.

This all happens automatically:
1. Once price action gets to PT1, the order sells 30% of my shares.
2. The other two portions are protected with a trailing stop for guaranteed profit.
3. When price action reaches PT2, the order sells 50% of my shares.
4. The remaining shares are protected with a trailing stop until I choose to adjust it.

According to my rules, no further action is required of me until PT2 is filled, and that can be days or weeks away. This adjustment can occur at my convenience, usually after hours. By using a trailing stop, I am guaranteed at least some more profit if the price goes even 1 penny higher from there.

In the example with ADI, my daily checkup routine shows me a bearish reversal candle that starts a normal flag. But it accelerates while closing below the 8-day. That's a warning to tighten my profit stop. I would have been taken out of the third portion with a profit during the next couple of days for a profit somewhere around 12-14% on PT3, and I'm satisfied with that outcome.

This is the most complicated portion of the entire system, and most people have never considered using these tools, so it's understandable if this is confusing at first. To see me walk through an example order, you can find a video tutorial in the bonus section at AutoPilotTraders.com/Print-Resources. Don't forget the coupon code PRINT100.

> **NOTE:** *On rare occasions, I may simplify this order by using a 1ˢᵗ Triggers 2 OCO instead of 3 OCOs, as described above. Normally, I only use this in situations where I'm fairly certain of getting a larger move in an entity, such as the seasonal spikes in the leveraged Gold ETF, NUGT.*
>
> *When I do this, I would take only a half position and split up the number of shares 50/50 for my exit targets.*
>
> *The other change I would make would be for PT1 to be 15-20%, adding a (-12.5%) trailing stop if triggered. For PT2, I would use a technical target or a Fib level, with the trailing stop waiting in the wings just in case it doesn't go that far.*

Peter Brandt says, "If you don't know precisely what signal is yours and how you will size and manage your position – Stop Trading!" Setting up your entry and exit parameters before the trade is critical in determining precisely how the trade orders will fit into your trading rules.

Your trading rules and tools are an insurance policy that capital is protected, and profits are taken based on having an "Edge." Establishing a routine for setting up and placing orders will reinforce the habit of following your rules. Plus, keeping a journal of this process greatly enhances a trader's ability to evaluate what went right and what went wrong with a specific trade or a season of trading.

This method of automating orders offers huge benefits in time-savings, trading consistency, and decision-making by controlling emotions. But like any tool, it won't work if you don't use it properly.

Because the way I use Conditional Orders is a bit more complex than traditional orders, it will take some time to learn and practice this skill. It can be easy when first learning to mix up order types or forget one of the pieces.

It takes just a little time and effort to learn this powerful tool. And you're almost guaranteed to make a losing trade with an instantaneous round trip if you try entering these orders with real money right away.

Practice these orders using a paper account or ThinkorSwim's On-Demand feature until you're comfortable using all of the tools of conditional orders consistently. It will save you money and stress!

I typically enter my initial order batches on Saturday or Sunday. As mentioned above, these entry order batches automatically cancel if they're not filled by Friday at market close.

The main reason entry orders are self-canceling is to ensure there are no surprise fills weeks after the orders are placed. Plus, it promotes following a sound trading routine.

Entry orders may be changed when the technical analysis warrants a change. A common example is if a stock finds support at a level higher than previously identified. This, of course, still has to pass the entry rules. Alternatively, you might cancel orders if the conditions change enough to void your PEP Routine analysis. Normally, I do not change entry orders until price action proves conditions have changed.

All it takes is checking for a couple of minutes each trading day.

Part of our Autopilot Trading service is a mid-week course correction that updates orders based on what the market is currently doing, so members get a heads-up even when they're busy.

Practice Trade Management daily. If a new support level is confirmed during the final hour of the day or after hours, raising a trailing stop may be in order if there is a significant difference between the existing stop loss or trailing stop and the new swing low. It only takes a few moments to look at the charts of current positions—and that few moments could save you a load of money and frustration.

You might also consider tightening stops if a trade is repeatedly bumping its head on resistance, if you see bearish reversal candles, or if momentum weakens. If you get all three with bearish divergence, I strongly suggest bringing up that stop.

When considering modifying trailing stops from the original plan, look at the stock, but also the overall market condition. If the indices are falling, they will tend to take 70-75% of stocks down also. In this case, it would be prudent to tighten the trailing stop to protect profits and capital. If your stop is hit, and the stock has proven to be stronger than the indices, look for a new setup.

Many times, traders will not re-enter a stock they've been stopped out of. This can be a tremendous missed opportunity, usually with a solid signal. Often, a strong trending stock will pull back just enough to trigger a PT3 trailing stop and "rest" while the market falls—only to provide a new PEP Setup while the broad market finds its own bottom. Learn to trade your system's signals, and it will take good care of you!

Review:

- Automation helps with both efficiency and psychology.
- You can automate most of your trade by bundling your entry order with "follow-up" exit orders.
- Be strategic with the conditions for your order. Add a time when unfilled orders will cancel themselves, or add a condition before the order is sent to hide it from Market Makers.
- Exit orders can be paired with a stop and target. One Cancels Other type orders will fill only the first side that's triggered.
- To review the concepts of order automation, watch a demo of my method using ThinkorSwim with the tutorials included with your purchase of the book at AutoPilotTraders.com/Print-Resources. Use the coupon code PRINT100.
- Plan time in your schedule to learn and practice order entry with paper trading or On-Demand.

CHAPTER EIGHTEEN

RECAP, CONCLUSION, AND THANK YOU

Most likely, you'll read this section before you have used the roadmap to attain the goal of one million dollars from trading. After all, we tried to make that target believable by putting it out ten years. So, if you choose to go down this road with us, put it in your plan, and maybe even in your calendar, to come back to this chapter as you approach that target.

Here's what I'd suggest after following the roadmap to your goal:

First, give yourself a huge congratulations. Celebrate the small successes along the way, but especially celebrate such a big achievement. Don't go crazy, but do something to treat yourself and those who have supported you. Take your family out for a nice dinner or take a day off from work to do something that you love. Maybe check off a bucket list item.

Next, chart a new plan to protect and continue growing your wealth. Here's an outline to consider.

Past a million dollars, it can start to become more difficult to get orders filled because of position size.

To protect most of your wealth, transfer it into trades with a longer-term perspective and less aggressive management or into other vehicles. Depending on your personal goals and style, that might look like moving into longer-term investing in the markets.

I don't mean traditional buy and hold. With the mastery you've attained, you can use the tools of the AutoPilot Trading Method and tweak the method. Make your trading decisions on a weekly or monthly chart instead of on a daily and intraday chart. That should get you into large positions when the market has been beaten down, allow you to ride most of the resulting bullish trend, and exit before the market moves into a new downtrend. You might need to adjust stop and target levels after some back testing.

You might also diversify that money into alternative investments, businesses, or property with a stable history. Real estate is a time-tested option that can create both cash flow and appreciation, though it will have its own learning curve, and you will need a new set of advisors and mentors. For a more passive real estate option, consider private lending or investing in the secondary mortgage market. This option primarily creates cash flow but is more passive than managing rental property. I have contacts in this industry if you'd like an introduction.

Commodities, precious metals, and collectibles are other popular alternative investments that can preserve or protect wealth, sometimes generate income, and may provide further options or flexibility for growth. With the added benefit that if society ever collapsed, you'd have something to trade for food. In the meantime, these types of assets may just bring a little more beauty to your life.

These days, there are new options to consider thanks to blockchain technology, like crypto or Non-Fungible Tokens

(NFTs). However, these look more speculative as of early 2023, based on potential regulatory schemes and the fundamental weakness of some offerings.

No doubt there are other alternative investments, but each one comes with its own set of rules and regulations, tax considerations, and expertise involved in their buying and selling. Do your due diligence and find appropriate help.

Here's the bottom line: if you were able to follow our roadmap to a tee (unlikely, I know, just from personal variances, taxes, etc.) or even relatively close, you would have just over one million dollars at year ten. Our original calculations came to $1,071,167.45.

Investing $870,000 of that money at the S&P's typical stated rate of return of 10% compounded annually, this long-term account would grow to $1.4 Million in five years, compounded only annually. Meanwhile, we could continue investing the remaining $200,000 using the AutoPilot Trading Method and make ourselves a new roadmap. Starting with $200,000 and adding $100 dollars per month at 40% per year compounded monthly, our active trading account would be back at $1.48 Million in those 5 years. While it took us ten years to turn our small nest egg into a million, we can almost triple that in just five years, even if we keep over 80% of it in traditionally geared investments.

If you're not doing the calculations yourself, at the end of five years your total account value would be $2,849,995.83 using these numbers.

At this point, you could rinse and repeat, more than doubling your money again in five years.

Or, having grown a passive nest egg over $2.6 million within the span of 15 years, you could take it easy. If invested at the industry-preferred rate of 10% per year, you could retire on an annual income of nearly $265,000.

Meanwhile, your remaining $200,000+ can be brought back up to $1 Million every five years with the AutoPilot Trading Method, continuing to grow both your wealth and your retirement income as long as you desire.

Again, this is an outline to consider, not a recommendation or iron-clad dictate. Your own lifestyle, financial decisions, and priorities mean that, at this point, you will be qualified and compensated enough to make your own choices.

At some point, your nest egg ought to be big enough for your personal needs and family needs, including a potential legacy for children and grandchildren. Most of us, when we are blessed with more than enough, feel the urge to give back and contribute. I hope that you will consider planning for that as part of your strategy—even before you reach that big goal. Some of that old wisdom I like says "A generous person will prosper; whoever refreshes others will be refreshed." [7]

For me, the entire endeavor of wealth-building is an effort to build God's kingdom and to see more resources being used for his mission and his glory. As a coach and teacher, I especially feel there is a desperate need for education that aligns with God's word and allows parents to teach according to their conscience. As an example, my personal wealth plans include an intent and goal to build a charitable trust up to the point that I can give scholarships to families choosing Christian homeschooling as an option to raise up the next generation for God's glory.

If you desire to leave a legacy of blessing for a deserving cause (religious or not), you might choose to fund a charitable trust with your trading proceeds and invest them at that conservative rate of 10%. I'm not a lawyer who can help

---

[7] Proverbs 11:25

with those plans, but with the right professional advice, it may be possible to structure such a charitable trust in a way that benefits your preferred philanthropic efforts while also paying you in your retirement years.

Again, you would need to get your advice from a qualified professional, but in theory, a two-million-dollar account set up as a charitable trust making 10% per year would have a budget of two hundred thousand dollars per year. If you were the sole employee or director, an income of one hundred thousand would not be out of the question as long as it's legal and ethical where you live. That means one hundred thousand for funding the efforts of the charitable trust every year.

With the right advisors at this stage—that is, the stage of financial freedom—you'll be able to come up with creative solutions to fit your goals, both personal and charitable. Thinking about wealth-building with this perspective gives it a lot more significance and meaning to me than just stuffing away as much money as I can for me and my loved ones. I get to build my Lord's kingdom, which, for me, is an even greater purpose, perhaps the most significant of my life.

⊦₊ϙ⊦ϙ

It's fun to dream about what might be with the possibilities laid out before you, but this entire roadmap begins with you deciding whether the AutoPilot Trading Method is right for you and whether you will put in the work to learn and execute with diligence and fortitude.

I truly believe this is a skill that most people *can* learn. However, the test of character and discipline needed to be highly successful at that skill is what decides whether you will make it or end up on the pile of former traders with blown up accounts.

Thank you for reading to this point. There's one more pillar that can help you become a great trader. Unfortunately, it's another item that many successful professionals, especially engineers, aren't eager to use. Will you be one of the few?

Take Action!

Dream a little. Plan out your roadmap to your first $1 Million if you haven't already.

Then, plan a few things for beyond that mile marker.

CHAPTER NINETEEN

PILLAR 6 – HOW TO GET MORE HELP

I developed the concept of pillars as a way to explain the need for a cohesive and complete system while talking to trading groups and coaching my own students. Originally, I listed only five, the ones we covered in the bulk of this book. In the past couple of years, I came to realize that the system alone, that is, the mechanics, indicators, parameters, and rules, is not enough to make a great trader.

I still believe great traders can be made, even if some are more naturally talented than others. But handing the system to the average person on the street will more likely result in failure, in my opinion, than success. The missing ingredient to turn the average person into a highly successful one in any endeavor is mentoring.

I could have read a thousand books and spent a lot of time in a flight simulator to learn about being a pilot. Maybe that would have given me enough skill to fly a small private plane, but with what I know even about that, I probably wouldn't have been safe. The shared expertise, and personalized instruction from former pilots is what gave me the ability to fly jets for the Navy. You probably have something in your own experience where you can see how you could have figured out how to do something, but having a mentor made you significantly better.

Studying with someone who has hundreds or thousands of repetitions at a particular skill will give you a broader and deeper knowledge than looking at hundreds or thousands of examples without taking action or without having the insight of someone who has successfully accomplished those things before.

Trading is no different. As we said at the beginning of the book, part of my reason for writing it is to encourage you.

I also said there that part of my reason for writing it was to give you a desire to hire us for our trading services and perhaps coaching and mentoring. I hope that the bulk of the information here has at least earned your acknowledgment that I would be capable in that endeavor. However, I'm realistic enough to recognize that my system isn't for everyone, and that even everyone who might be interested in my system may not be a good fit as my student. I wouldn't even have all of the time necessary to personally train everyone who might want to use our system.

Again, those reasons are packed into my motivation for writing the book. Also, I still hope to help you, even if we never get to work together in a more personal way. So, this final chapter will include a few resources to give you additional help, whether from me or from another source.

For buying this book, you already have a list of bonuses and follow-up resources available at AutoPilotTraders.com/Print-Resources. On that page, you'll find further examples of my set up and trade methodology, in-depth videos explaining how I enter orders, information about how I sort stocks to get to the cream of the crop, the trade journal and trade log published on Amazon, a special video explaining how to use ThinkorSwim's On-Demand simulator for back testing and training, and a special video on trading opportunities in a bear market.

The coupon code PRINT100 will get you free access to all of it.

Other Books

Books are another great way to get training and education from highly successful experts. My three favorites are *How to Make Money Trading Stocks* by William O'Neill, *Think and Trade like a Champion* by Mark Minervini, and *Trend Trading for a Living* by Dr. William Carr.

Other very helpful options are *The Mental Game of Trading* by Jared Tendler and *The Trading Mindwheel* by Michael Lamothe. These two focus more on mindset and psychology than on mechanics or strategy. Studying these classics would give you an incredible base of knowledge and allow you to evaluate what type of trading methodology might work best for you. You might decide to follow their recommendations, and that's perfect for some people.

Find a whole list of my recommendations at AutoPilot-Traders.com/ReadingList.

I would also be more than happy to welcome you into the ranks of Autopilot Traders. I'm happy as long as you're getting good, reliable training.

Trade Your Way to Freedom Master Course

If you enjoyed this book but feel like a different format would help you master these skills sooner, check out the Trade Your Way to Freedom Master Course. The course covers all the concepts in this book in bite-sized videos, but allows for more examples and the benefit of seeing visually how things work and play out. There's also a workbook and extra bonuses to help you learn the AutoPilot Method.

Find it at: AutoPilotTraders.com/TYWTFMasterCourse

Autopilot Trading Service

If you're excited about the method, but you just don't feel you have enough time to learn and implement – or if you struggle with confidence in your ability to trade the system successfully— consider my AutoPilot Trading Service.

The AutoPilot Trading Service uses the methods described in this book and boils everything down into a handful of trade signals every week. Subscribers receive five trades that I intend to take on growth stocks and two trades from our stable of leveraged ETFs. The initial setups are highlighted on the weekend, and I send out any updates to that plan during the week if the market condition changes.

Learn more about the AutoPilot Trading Service at AutoPilotTraders.com/Membership. Use coupon code FREEDOM10 to get a discount for buying the book.

Other Autopilot Related Services

You can also find some free and low-cost options to continue learning from me at AutoPilotTraders.com/Catalog, like a mini-course on the PEP Routine, and my weekly free newsletter.

There's also my YouTube channel, where you can find weekly market analysis and evergreen trading tips at:

YouTube.com/@AutopilottradingMarketTechTalk.

Mentoring

If you are ready to challenge yourself with a full year of deep training in the systems, routines, and mentality of the AutoPilot System, I invite you to apply to our group Mentoring Program. It focuses on 5 elements:

1. Building the habits of trading
2. Learning the AutoPilot system
3. Practicing while you learn
4. Group Mentoring calls
5. A Community of traders on the same journey

There are no special secrets in this group, but you would get live instruction and feedback, detailed examples and training, and the valuable opportunity to ask questions on any points that are unclear to you. But this program is only available by application!

If you would like to learn directly from me in implementing the AutoPilot Trading Method for yourself, apply at AutoPilotTraders.com/Apply.

Thank you again for picking up my book. I sincerely hope that it helps you learn to trade more successfully, more confidently, and leads you on a path to freedom. I salute your efforts and hope that you learn to become a wise and profitable trader!

APPENDIX

Candlesticks – The 7 Patterns I use.

These are the candlestick patterns that I focus on after researching which ones were common and significantly predictive of a reversal.

The specific reversal percentages are from Bulkowski's book, *The Encyclopedia of Chart Patterns*, and his blog, ThePatternSite.com. Both are great resources.

One thing to keep in mind is that these percentages reflect the probability of a reversal any time a valid candlestick pattern appears. The probabilities are only counted for the candlestick pattern by itself. They do not take into consideration the other elements of our PEP routine. When these patterns appear near support/resistance and with momentum turning, the odds of a reversal increase.

Your own interpretation can still affect how well you trade these in each circumstance and should improve with practice.

For more details on how I read these candlesticks, check out the video that is included on the book's resources page at AutoPilotTraders.com/Print-Resources. (Coupon Code PRINT100)

6 Primary Patterns

Hammer / Hanging Man

Probability of a reversal: 66% / 59%

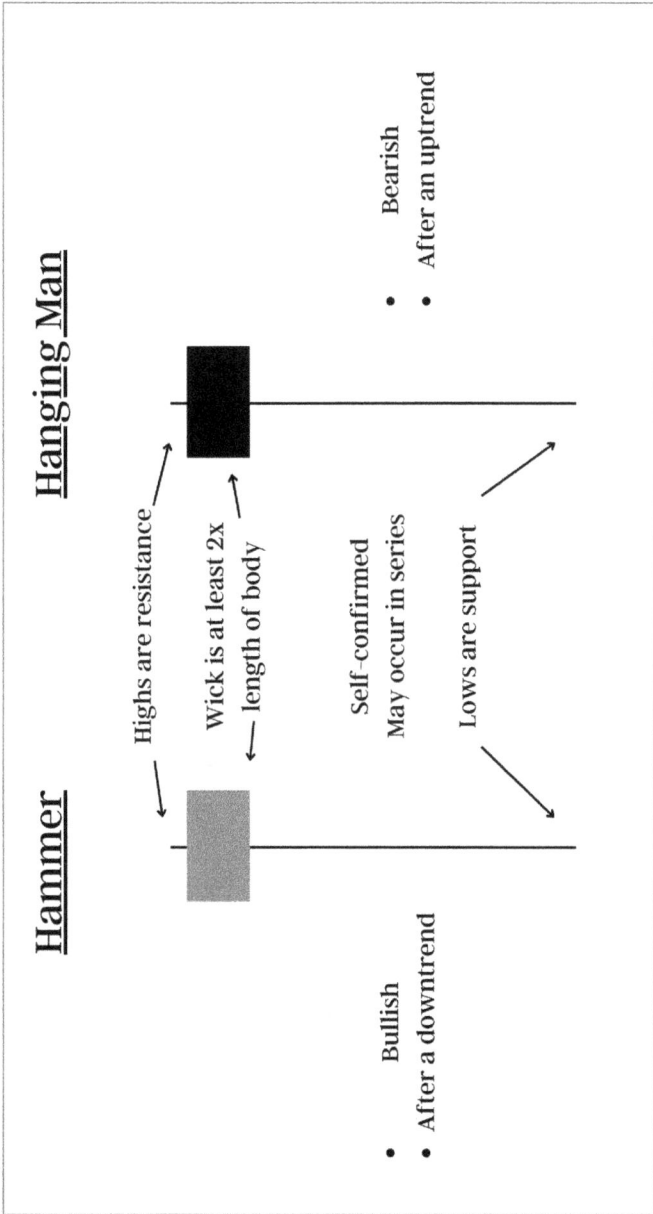

Shooting Star / Inverted Hammer
Probability of a reversal: 65% / 59%

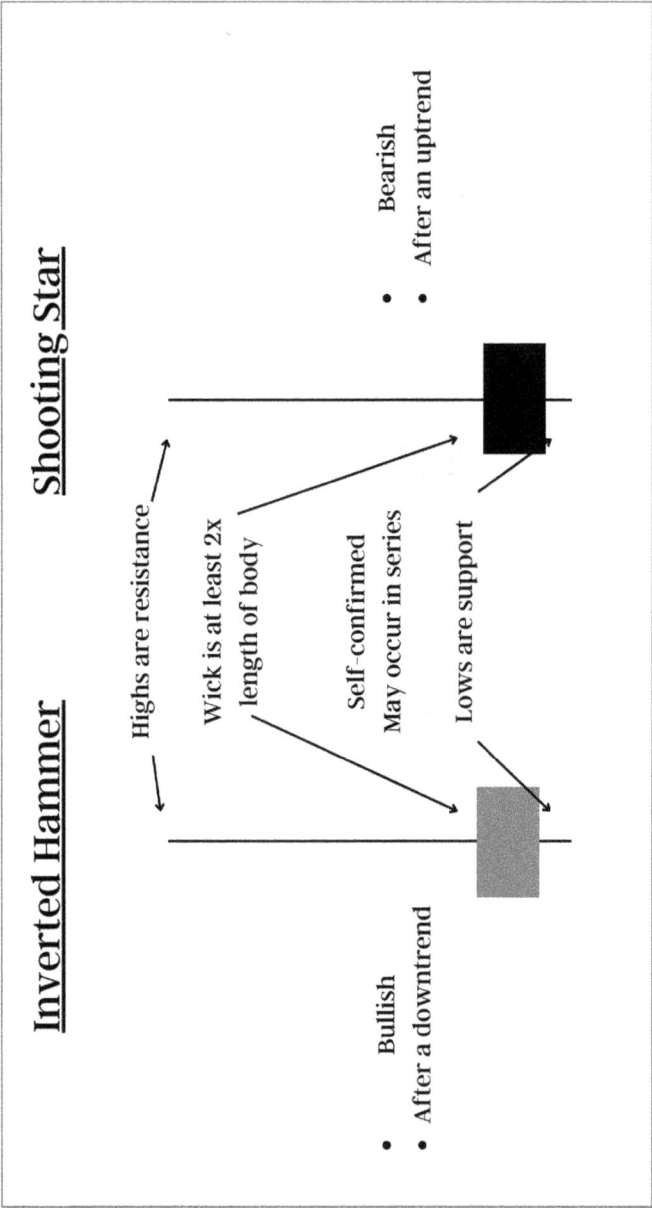

Engulfing Pattern
Probability of a reversal: 63% / 79%

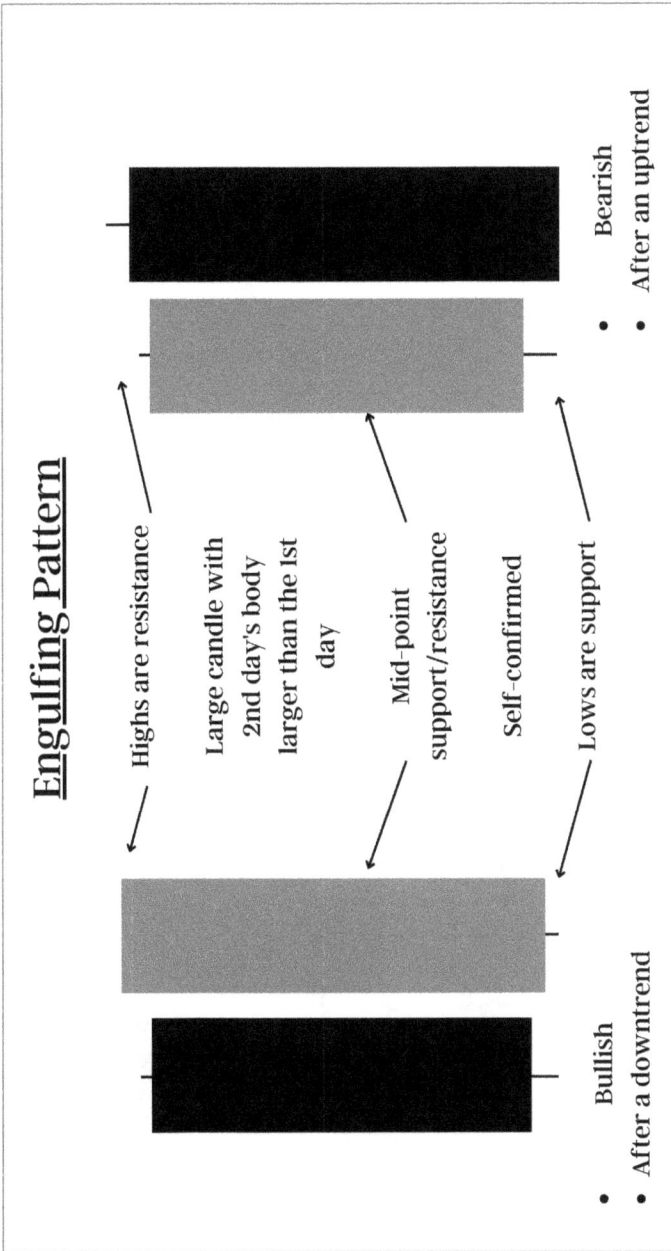

Engulfing Pattern

- Bearish
- After an uptrend

- Bullish
- After a downtrend

Highs are resistance

Large candle with
2nd day's body
larger than the 1st
day

Mid-point
support/resistance

Self-confirmed

Lows are support

Piercing Line / Dark Cloud
Probability of a reversal: 64% / 60%

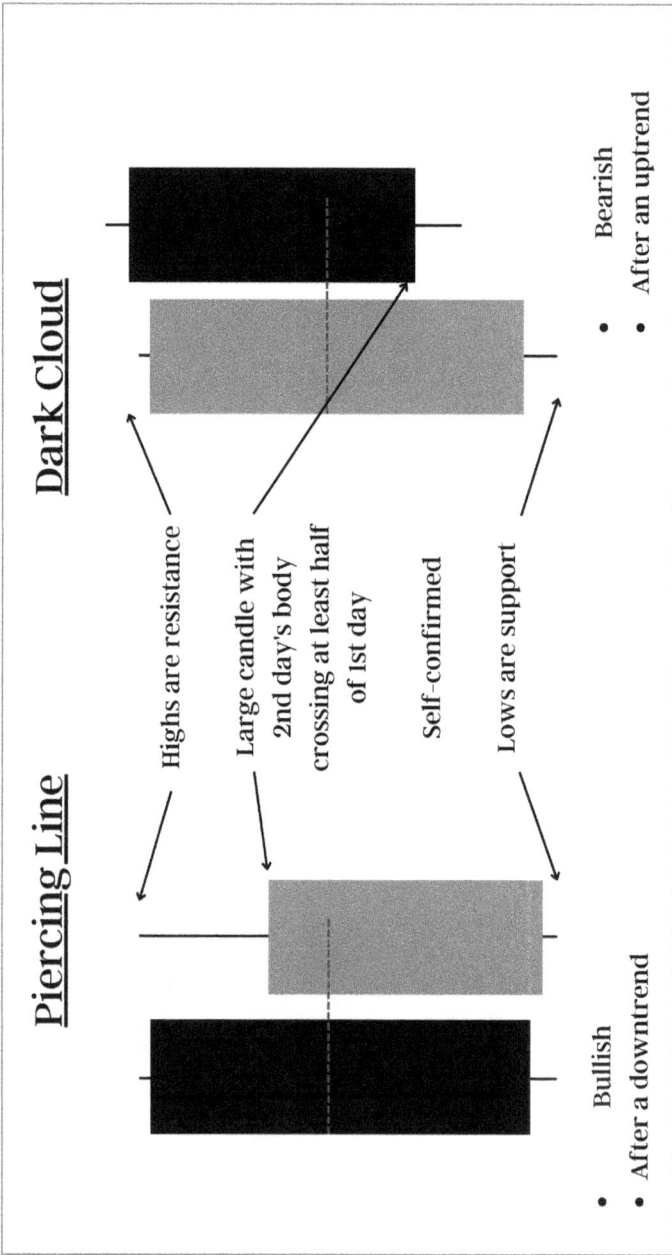

Morning Star / Evening Star
Probability of a reversal: 78% / 72%

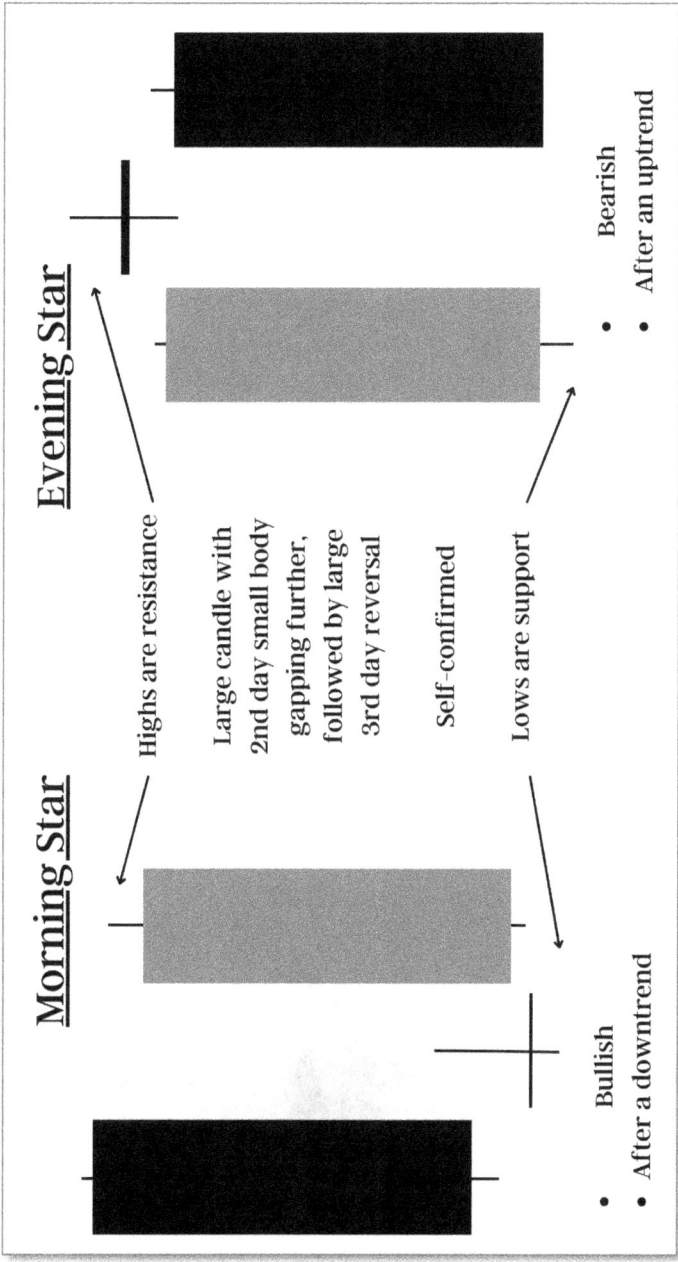

Evening Star

- Bearish
- After an uptrend

Morning Star

- Bullish
- After a downtrend

Highs are resistance

Large candle with 2nd day small body gapping further, followed by large 3rd day reversal

Self-confirmed

Lows are support

Harami
Probability of a reversal: 53% / 53%

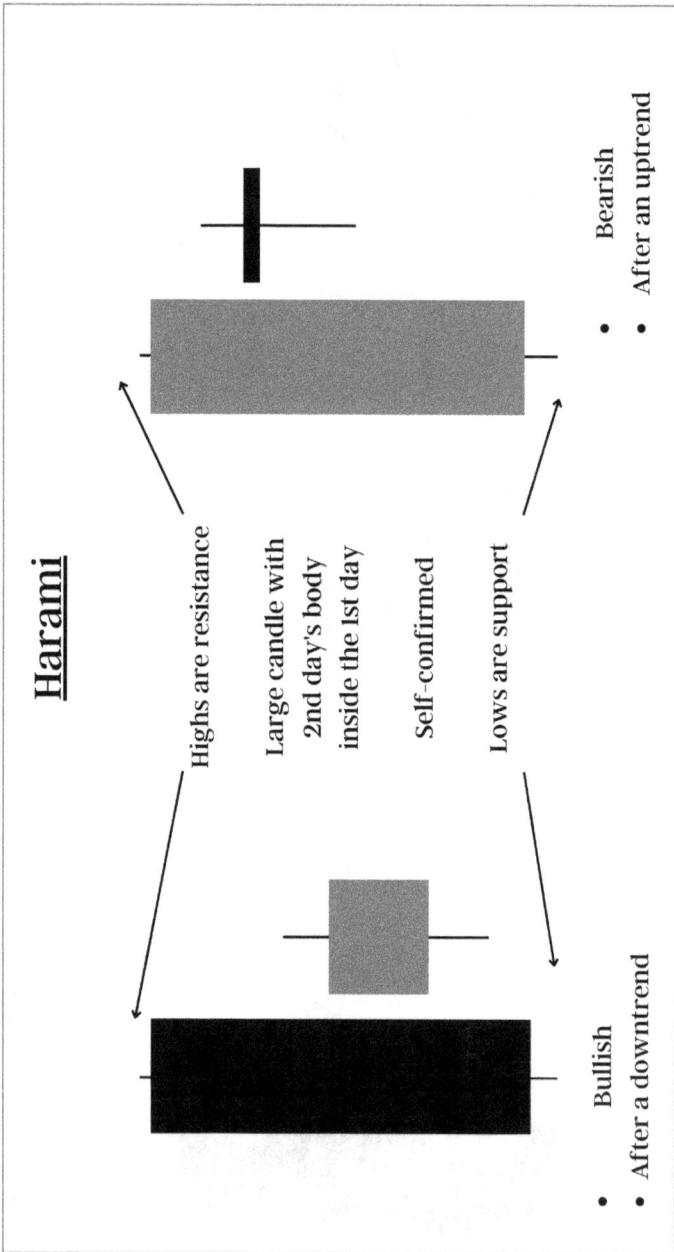

Harami

- Highs are resistance
- Large candle with 2nd day's body inside the 1st day
- Self-confirmed
- Lows are support

- Bearish
- After an uptrend

- Bullish
- After a downtrend

1 Indecision Pattern

Doji / Spinning Tops: Buyers and Sellers Fighting for Control, suggesting a 50/50 chance on the next direction.

Doji / Spinning Top

Represent indecision

Doji have almost no body-open and close are nearly the same

Spinning tops have smaller than average bodies

Often occur in clusters during consolidation or testing @ support/resistance

AutoPilot Triggers Cheat Sheet

Here's a quick-reference of the elements of our triggers. You can also find a downloadable version on the resource page.

AutoPilot Trigger Cheat Sheet

Autopilot TRADING

PEP Routine:
1. Price Near Support
2. Confirmed Reversal Candlesticks
3. Momentum (TSI) turning

Trigger 1: Early
Strong support necessary.
High probability candlesticks preferred.
Momentum: starting to bend, but not yet turned up.
Enter 10-20 cents above strongest support level

Trigger 2: Momentum Turn
Strong support necessary.
High probability candlesticks preferred.
Momentum: turned up from Oversold condition, may have show positive divergence.
Enter 10-20 cents above support - check 30 minute chart for VAZs

Trigger 3: Close Above 8-Day
Already bounced from support, 8-day becomes support.
May have previous candlestick signals.
Momentum: already turned up, may show positive divergence.
Enter near the close of day or 10-20 cents above 8-day the following days.

Trigger 4: Flags in Existing Uptrend
Support for short term pullback flags may be horizontal, uptrend line or MAs.
Candle-stick signals may appear near bottom of flags.
Momentum: already turned up, may be pulling back and bouncing like price.
Enter 10-20 cents above support or MAs.

Special Condition A: Large Candles Close Above 8-Day
Hidden support on very large candles may be stronger than 8-day.
May have previous candlestick signals. Check 30 minute charts for VAZs
Momentum: likely already turned up, may show positive divergence.
On the following days, enter 10-20 cents above strongest hidden support.

Special Condition B: Gap Higher
Short pullback ends in doji type candle; then gaps higher at open.
Often occurs around earnings.
Momentum: already turned up, may be pulling back and bouncing like price.
Use trigger 4 above to enter on flag pullbacks to support or MAs.

ACKNOWLEDGMENTS

This journey of writing *Trade Your Way to Freedom* has been nothing short of a remarkable experience, and it's only fitting to begin by acknowledging the foundation that underlies it all. Two Bible passages, Proverbs 3:5-10 and Deuteronomy 8:18, have been my guiding lights, shaping the very essence of my life and this book.

Proverbs 3:5-10 teaches us to "Trust in the Lord with all your heart and lean not on your own understanding." It reminds us that our paths are directed by a higher wisdom, which resonates profoundly with the trading principles I've shared. Deuteronomy 8:18 NIV, which reminds us that it is God who "gives you the ability to produce wealth," has been a constant reminder of the divine grace that has touched my life.

With humility and gratitude, I begin these acknowledgments by recognizing how God's presence has shaped every word and concept within these pages.

In the world of trading, it's crucial to stand on the shoulders of giants, and I've been fortunate to have some remarkable guides along this path. First, I want to acknowledge the profound influence of William O'Neil, the visionary founder of Investor's Business Daily (IBD), and the architect of the CANSLIM trading process. His ground-breaking methodology served as the launchpad for much of my initial work with the Active Trend Trading System which is now a strong part of the AutoPilot Trading System. Mr. O'Neil's company has consistently provided me with meticulously vetted stock candidates, allowing me to focus on what I do best—Technical Analysis.

Another significant influence on my trading journey has been Stephen Bigalow, both as a coach and mentor. His guidance on properly utilizing Candlestick Trading Patterns has been instrumental in refining my trading strategies. Additionally, I must pay homage to my well-worn 9th edition of Edwards and Magee's *Technical Analysis of Stock Trends*, a timeless resource that has been a steadfast companion throughout the years.

Mark Douglas' book, *Trading in the Zone*, deserves special mention. It played a pivotal role in liberating me to adopt the mindset of a winner, teaching me the importance of mastering my psychology in the trading arena.

While building my system, I took the best of what they had to offer so I could achieve a Clear and Simple Approach to Swing Trading Success.

A book takes shape through the collective effort of many hands, and I'm profoundly thankful for those who have been instrumental in its refinement. To my team of diligent beta readers: Anil Parikh, Barbara Nigh, Jim Lee, Mark Langenbacher, Nicole Shipman, and Rocco Musumeche, your invaluable feedback and attention to detail have brought clarity and precision to every page. Your commitment to excellence has been the bedrock upon which this work stands, and I extend my heartfelt appreciation to each one of you.

I would also like to extend my deepest gratitude to Michael Lamothe, who kindly agreed to write the foreword for this book. Mike, my friend, your unwavering support and camaraderie have been a source of inspiration and encouragement that words cannot adequately capture. You've touched my journey in ways that extend far beyond the pages of this book, and I am profoundly grateful for your friendship and mentorship.

To all the readers who have embarked on this journey to master the AutoPilot Trading System, your investment in learning and growing as traders is a testament to your determination and commitment. It's your unwavering dedication that fuels the essence of this book, and for that, I am profoundly grateful. I hope that the strategies and insights you discover within these pages provide you with the clarity and simplicity you seek on your path to Swing Trading Success. Your trust in this work is deeply appreciated, and I look forward to sharing in your successes as you navigate the intricate world of trading.

A heartfelt and enormous thank you goes out to my son, Brandon, whose dedication and expertise as both an author and editor have breathed life into this book. His remarkable talents have contributed to what I believe is one of the finest Swing Trading Books ever written. I am immensely proud of the collaboration that led to this accomplishment.

To my lovely bride, Michele, your unwavering support through the highs and lows of my journey in learning to trade has been the bedrock of my determination. You are not just my rock, but my greatest inspiration.

Aloha and blessings to all who are on this incredible journey of learning Swing Trading.

ABOUT THE AUTHOR

Dennis Wilborn spent over twenty years in the United States Navy, first as a pilot and then in the Seabees, or Naval engineering core.
He followed that up with over ten years in corporate America building cellular networks.
His interest in stocks and investing formed after learning about mutual funds as a young teenager. Seeing a chart of compounding returns gave him a lifelong desire to master trading and build wealth.
Dennis has taught in stock clubs and trading groups since 2006, eventually coming to lead the Bay Area Money Makers or BAMM in San Jose, California. That's now a virtual Meetup you can join for free at Meetup.com/bammibd.
In 2012, Dennis began coaching and teaching small groups of traders professionally through his company, Active Trend Trading.
Since then, his Active Trend Trading system has a strong track record of beating the S&P 500, with average annual returns of about 36%.

After fine-tuning his proprietary method to automate trades, he rebranded the business into AutoPilot Trading in 2022.

In the last ten years, he's found he loves teaching and coaching just as much as trading.

Trade Your Way to Freedom is Dennis' first book, written to reach busy professionals with a system they can use to build wealth while they're still working full time.

Learn more about Dennis and his wealth building system and services at AutoPilotTraders.com.

He lives in Hawai'i with his wife of almost 50 years.

SPECIAL OFFER

As a Thank You for purchasing this book, you can get 10% off my premium AutoPilot Trading Service at

AutoPilotTraders.com/Membership

Use the coupon code FREEDOM10

The AutoPilot Trading Service gives you my exact trade parameters for the best opportunities in the market each week. You'll get the stocks I'm trading, with my PEP Routine Analysis, as well as the exact entry and exit orders I'm looking to trade each week with the same methods described in this book.